MODAL VOICINGS FOR GUITAR

RICK PECKHAM

To access audio and video visit:
www.halleonard.com/mylibrary

Enter Code
"7268-2666-2163-0925"

RECORDING

Guitar: Rick Peckham
Bass: Fernando Huergo
Drums: Michael Clarke
Engineer: Peter Kontrimas

BERKLEE PRESS

Editor in Chief: Jonathan Feist
Senior Vice President of Online Learning and Continuing Education/CEO of Berklee Online: Debbie Cavalier
Vice President of Enrollment Marketing and Management: Mike King
Vice President of Academic Strategy: Carin Nuernberg
Editorial Assistant: Brittany McCorriston

ISBN 978-0-87639-203-4

1140 Boylston Street
Boston, MA 02215-3693 USA
(617) 747-2146

Visit Berklee Press Online at
www.berkleepress.com

Study music online at
online.berklee.edu

DISTRIBUTED BY

HAL•LEONARD®
7777 W. BLUEMOUND RD. P.O. BOX 13819
MILWAUKEE, WISCONSIN 53213

Visit Hal Leonard Online
www.halleonard.com

Berklee Press, a publishing activity of Berklee College of Music, is a not-for-profit educational publisher.
Available proceeds from the sales of our products are contributed to the scholarship funds of the college.

CONTENTS

ACKNOWLEDGMENTS

I wish to thank all of the musicians and educators who've taught me everything I've learned over the past fifty years or so. Thousands of recordings, performances, transcriptions, collaborations, and lessons have helped me to gain a closer relationship with the ever-fascinating world of music. Special thanks to Jack Petersen and Rich Matteson for leading the way for me at a critical time in my professional life, and to similarly inspired colleagues with whom I've worked at Berklee College of Music, especially Larry Baione and Jim Kelly. Most thanks of all to my wife, Anne Peckham.

PREFACE

Like water and ice, scales and chords can be seen as different forms of the same element. Anyone who can play a scale can learn to build chords from that scale. Anyone who can play a chord can find a scale that will fit the sound.

Guitarists have long had a love/hate relationship with music theory and chord/scale theory in particular. Patient, persistent study will lead to understanding.

Every guitarist who seeks to improve needs to be able to teach themselves new material, and just as importantly, to have the ability to coach themselves to attain a level of fluency with regard to any concept. You have to coach the new things that you learn to the level that you feel them. You need to be able to drill and practice your way to fluency.

The best music teachers are able to spawn the best musician/teacher/coaches—developing musicians who have learned to teach and coach themselves to higher levels of understanding and performance. It's my goal to help you to be able to learn new ways of looking at modal elements. I want you to learn this material to the extent that you hear and feel it helping you to enhance your ability to collaborate with others with their musical vision and to help you to realize your own.

—Rick Peckham, 2020

ABOUT THE VIDEOS AND AUDIO FILES

To access the accompanying videos and audio examples for these lessons, visit www.halleonard.com/mylibrary and enter the code found on the first page of this book. This will grant you instant access to every example. Examples with accompanying media are marked with these icons:

Video

Audio

CHAPTER 1

Reinforcing Form through Chordal Accompaniment

Prior to exploring specific voicing content, a quick discussion of form as it applies to the chordal accompanist will be helpful. The concept of "form" is essential to the highest level of chordal accompaniment. Pianist Ray Santisi (1933 to 2014) taught at Berklee from 1957 until the end of his life, fifty-seven years later. Among his many accomplishments, he played with Charlie Parker in the 1950s. My favorite quote from Ray: "Form is the invisible language of musicians."

Making use of larger arcs, building 4-bar phrases into larger paragraphs (8-bar, 12-bar, 16-bar, 32-bar, etc.), is essential to performing the act of effective accompaniment. Musicians make use of phrases in multiples of four as a grid, or framework, for tension and release.

Listening to "So What" by Miles Davis on *Kind of Blue* (1959) and "Impressions" by John Coltrane on *Impressions* (1963), it's possible to hear the 32-bar AABA form boiled down to its essence. The chord progressions of these two pieces are, of course, identical, involving Dmin7 in the A sections and E♭min7 in the B section. If you're in an A section, you're playing Dmin7; if you're in a B, it's E♭min7. For players, it's a challenge to keep the form on track. Marking the double-bars clearly is the way that the rhythm section expresses the invisible language of musicians.

1, 2

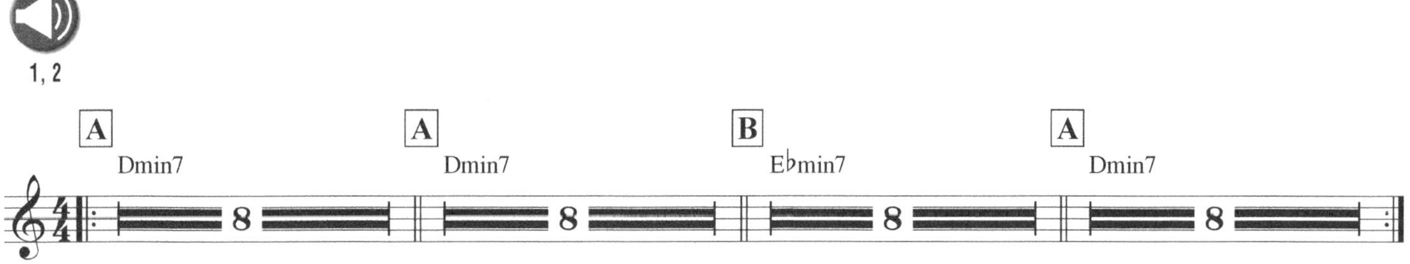

FIG. 1.1. "So What/Impressions" Form

This architecture can be seen as analogous to the agogic stress found in the beats of a 4/4 bar. Although the rhythmic emphasis in jazz is on 2 and 4, the strength of each beat of the 4/4 bar is seen as follows:

FIG. 1.2. Agogic Stress

Harmonic changes, or chordal attacks, occur most frequently on beat 1, or on beats 1 and 3. Composers put chord changes on these beats, making seldom use of beats 2 and 4 for this purpose.

To enable players to keep the AABA form together, it can be helpful to imagine this model of agogic stress as a way to think of, and feel, each of the double bars leading into the larger 8-bar segments.

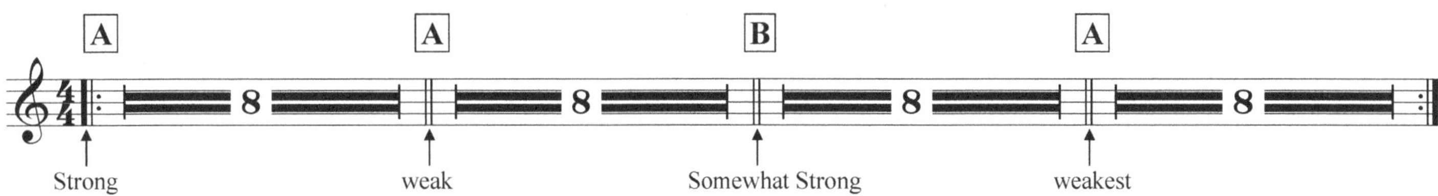

FIG. 1.3. Agogic Stress AABA Form

The most dramatic points of AABA occur on the top of the form (first A) and at the bridge (B section). When listening to these recordings with a classroom of students, I have the group clap once on the top of the form and on the bridge, and snap their fingers once on the second A and last A.

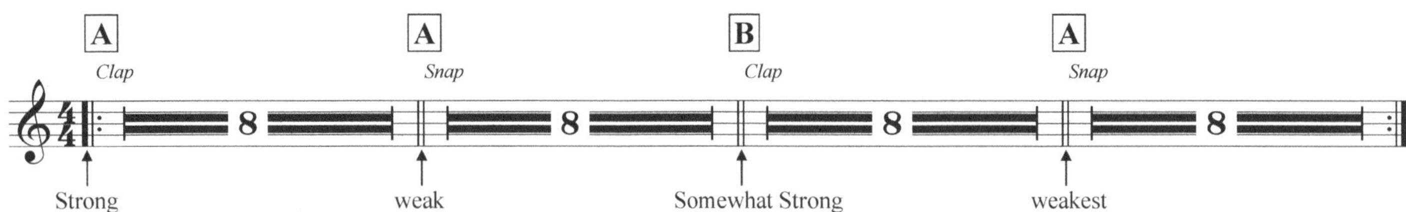

FIG. 1.4. Agogic Stress Claps and Snaps

Listen to these recordings, and mark the formal sections with claps and snaps, noticing the way that the drummer and pianist mark the sections with varying level of emphasis. The top of the form and the bridge are brought out with louder attacks, while the second A and last A are much more lightly marked.

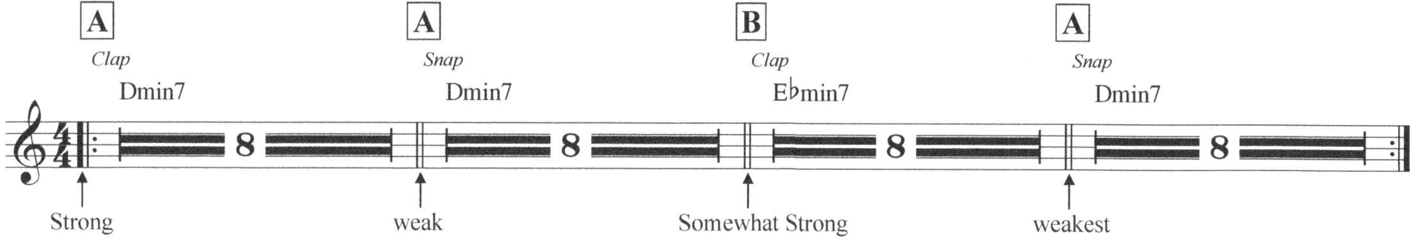

FIG. 1.5. Agogic Stress with Chords

We will be working with chord voicings, but consistent listening to great recordings will speed up your progress, while making the journey more enjoyable, in addition to adding to your ability to feel the music. See chapter 6, "Quartal Voicings on the 'So What/ Impressions' Progression" for specific voicing information to allow you to play along.

We are going to build up some vocabulary first.

CHAPTER 2

D Dorian in Fourths

Quartal harmony uses diatonic fourths as a means of producing interesting sounds from the diatonic major scale. The Dorian mode consists of the notes of the diatonic major scale from second degree to second degree an octave higher.

The birth of modal music in jazz involved quartal voicings. Many credit Bill Evans for bringing the harmony from the classical music style of impressionism to jazz. McCoy Tyner made this harmonic approach into a cornerstone of his music, and others followed suit.

Chords based on triads have a sense of tonal gravity and directly reflect functional harmony. Triadic harmony consists of an easy-to-follow arc, making it easy to hear a chord's root and chord quality. With chords based on fourths, there is less clarity with regard to root and chordal identity. The pull from one chord to the next seems much less like harmonic resolution than an exploration of harmonic colors. Each static chord stands independent—in its own atmosphere. The static chord is allowed to explore its own extended harmonic identity through the variously ordered notes of the home mode. You can enjoy the way it makes you feel, as opposed to easily following predictable resolutions. This is one of the defining characteristics of modal jazz, and we will explore quartal voicings as well as other modal structures throughout this book.

Here are the notes of the C major scale. From C to C, the scale is C major; the same notes, from D to D, yield the D Dorian mode. The note B is included here (at the beginning) to enable us to build fourth voicings in the next stage of this discussion.

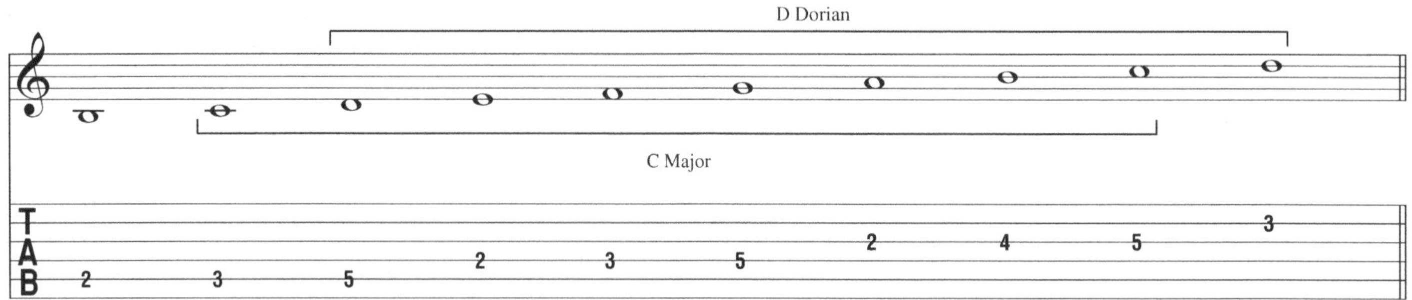

FIG. 2.1. D Dorian Scale

The term "Dorian voicings" frequently refers to the voicings of the major scale, starting on the second degree, played in diatonic fourths. In figure 2.2, we're starting with the root of the D Dorian scale, then traveling down the scale in fourth intervals, resulting in a voicing DAEB from the highest pitch to lowest. In a seven-note scale, it might be easiest to start from a tone, then skip two scale notes to find the next note, a diatonic fourth below it.

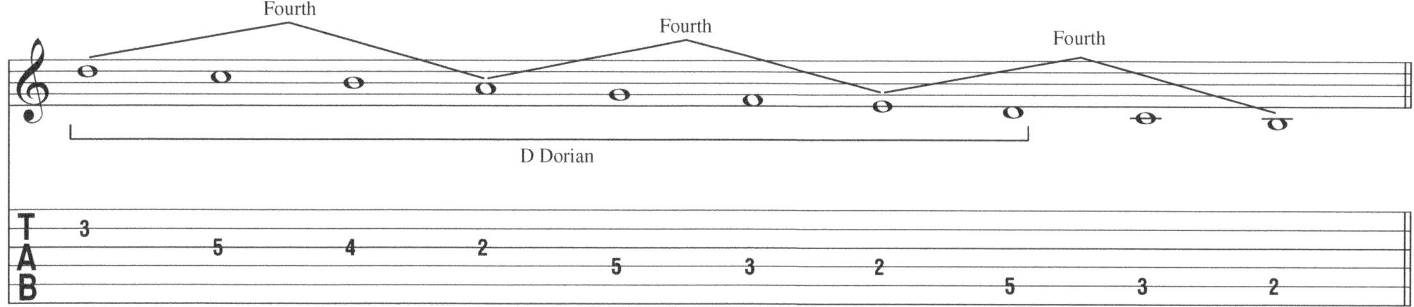

FIG. 2.2. Dorian in Fourths

This gives us the first voicing demonstrated here, in second position on strings ⑤ ④ ③ ②. Let's follow this voicing up the neck, sticking to the notes of D Dorian (or C major). Notice that some of the chords most prominently use a straight barre shape and others don't. Some of the voicings feature an augmented fourth—at first dissonant to the ear, but vital to the distinctive color of Dorian voicings.

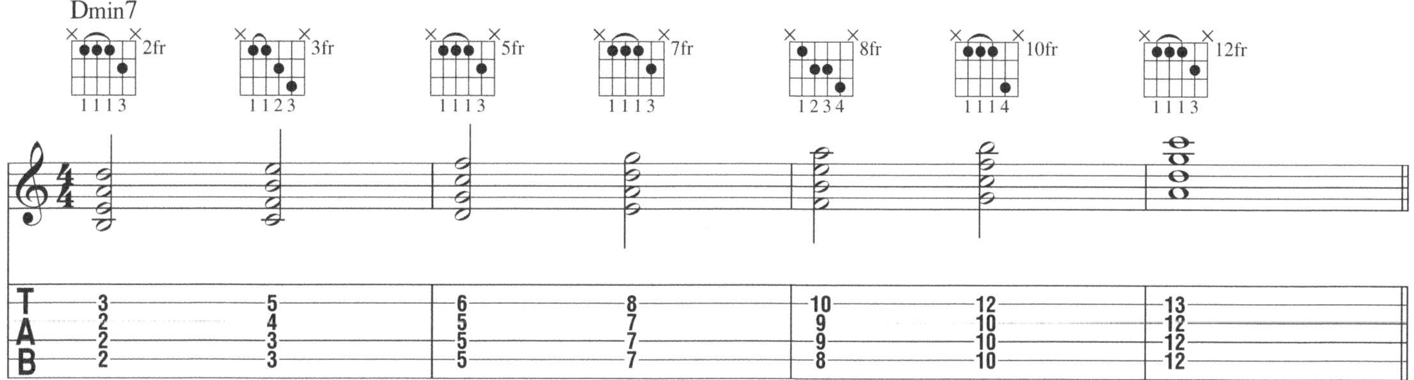

FIG. 2.3. Dorian Up Strings ⑤ ④ ③ ②

It's possible to find several string sets for the Dorian shapes, but the next logical location might be strings ④ ③ ② ①.

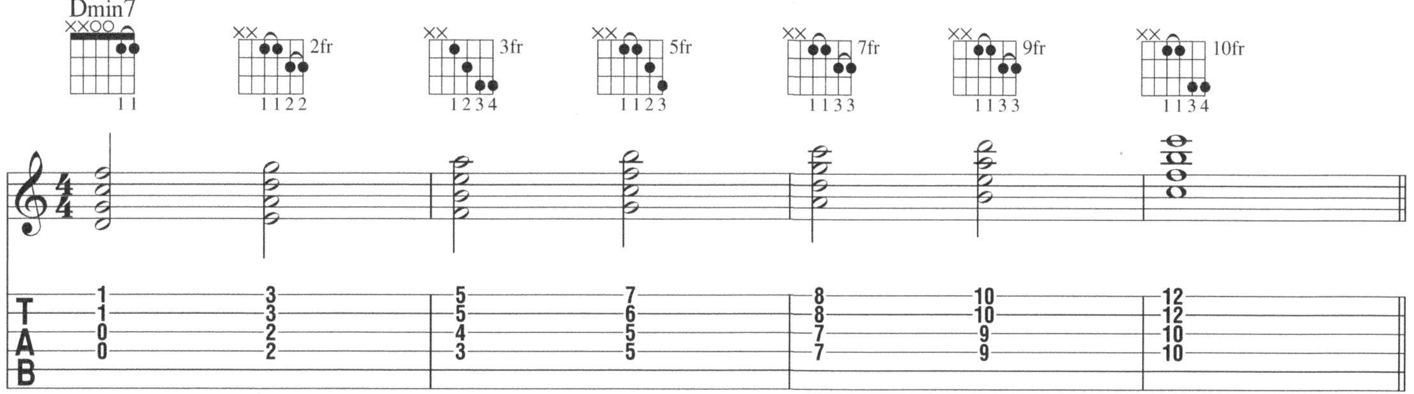

FIG. 2.4. Dorian Up Strings ④ ③ ② ①

Mixing the string sets yields some interesting sets of sounds, and some mental and technical challenges—essential to a thorough understanding of the set of colors. As a matter of ease and convenience, guitarists frequently stick to one string set while playing these shapes, producing somewhat predictable sounds. Mixing string groups will add to variety and cut down on predictability. Let's mix things up with the use of a broken pattern, moving through this diatonic material in the following way.

Up	Up	Down	Up
Diatonic 3rd	Diatonic 2nd	Diatonic 3rd	Diatonic 2nd

Here's what that would sound like, starting with D as the top note on the second set of four strings.

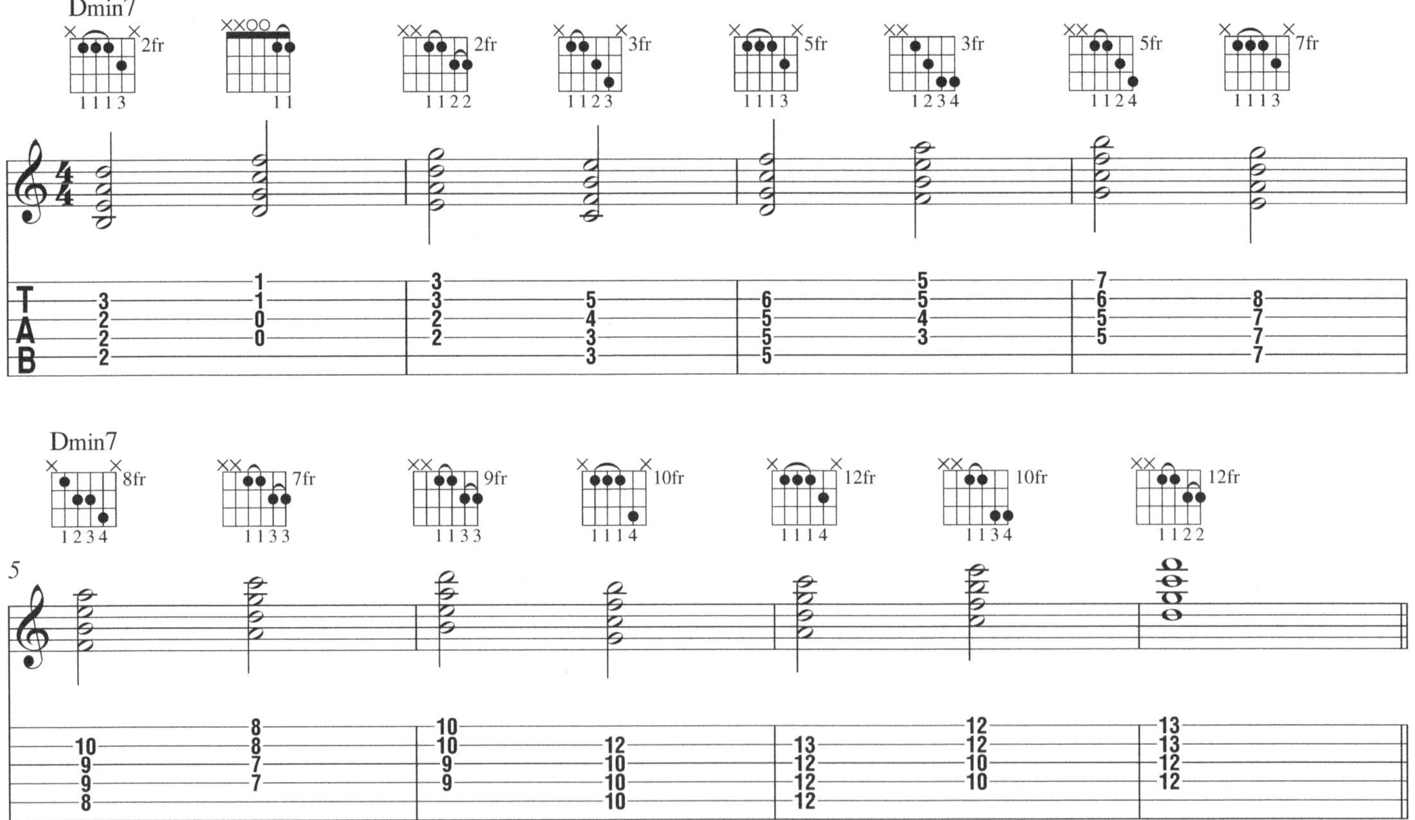

FIG. 2.5. D Dorian Broken Pattern

It's good to know a lot of things, but it's even better to know how to use a few things in a lot of different ways. Fluency with basic concepts, with ready access to practical uses, can be much more useful than a less-clear grasp of disparate groups of information.

Let's do some further work with the Dorian voicings. As discussed and demonstrated in the video, play through the D Dorian voicings on ⑤ ④ ③ ② and ④ ③ ② ①.

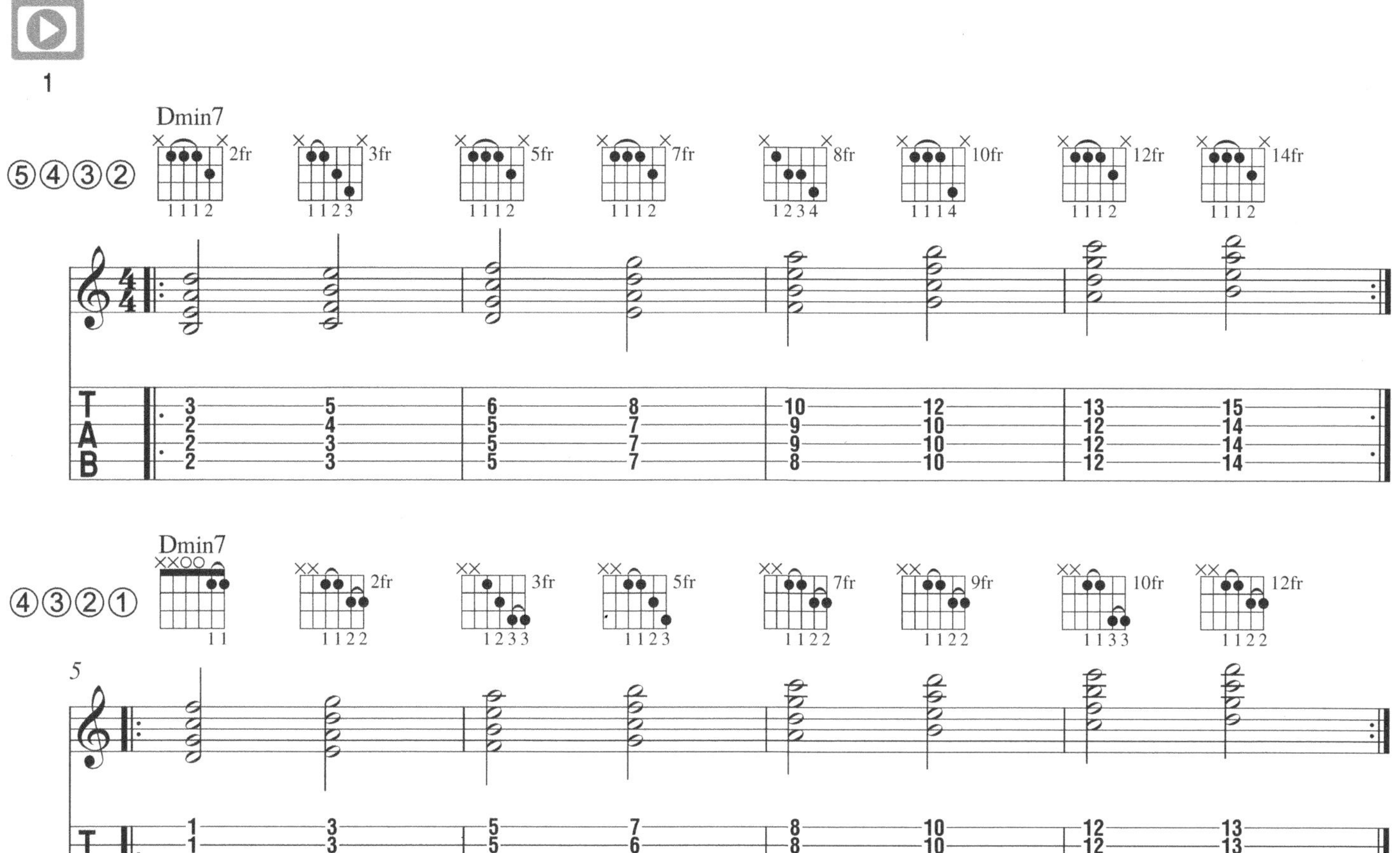

FIG. 2.6. Dorian in Fourths

Mixing up the string sets, play through the following sequence.

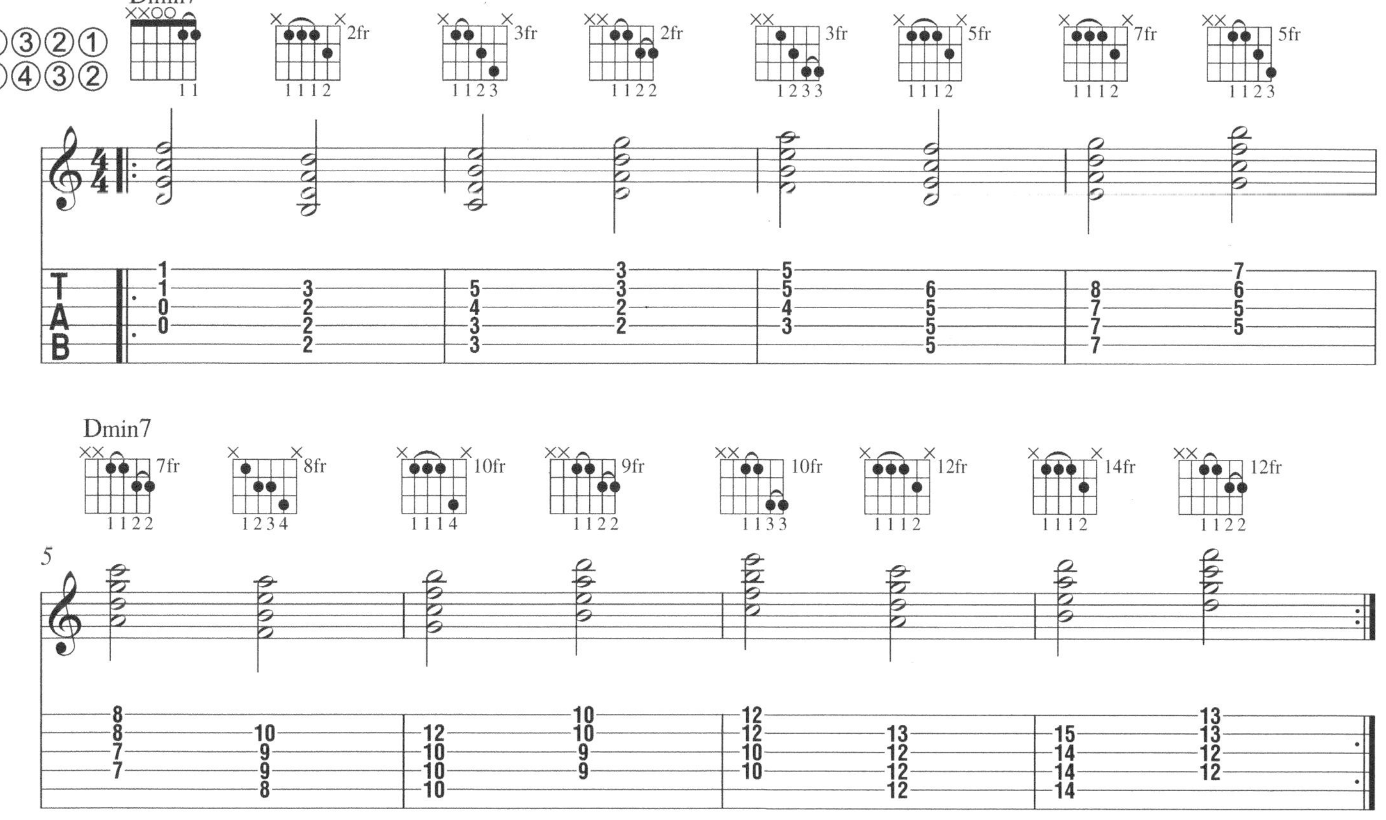

FIG. 2.7. D Dorian/C Major Mixing String Sets

Video tracks 2 through 8 present several variations, intended as a way to gain some fluency with the shapes. Here's the first variation presented with a bass line that outlines a D Dorian sound.

2

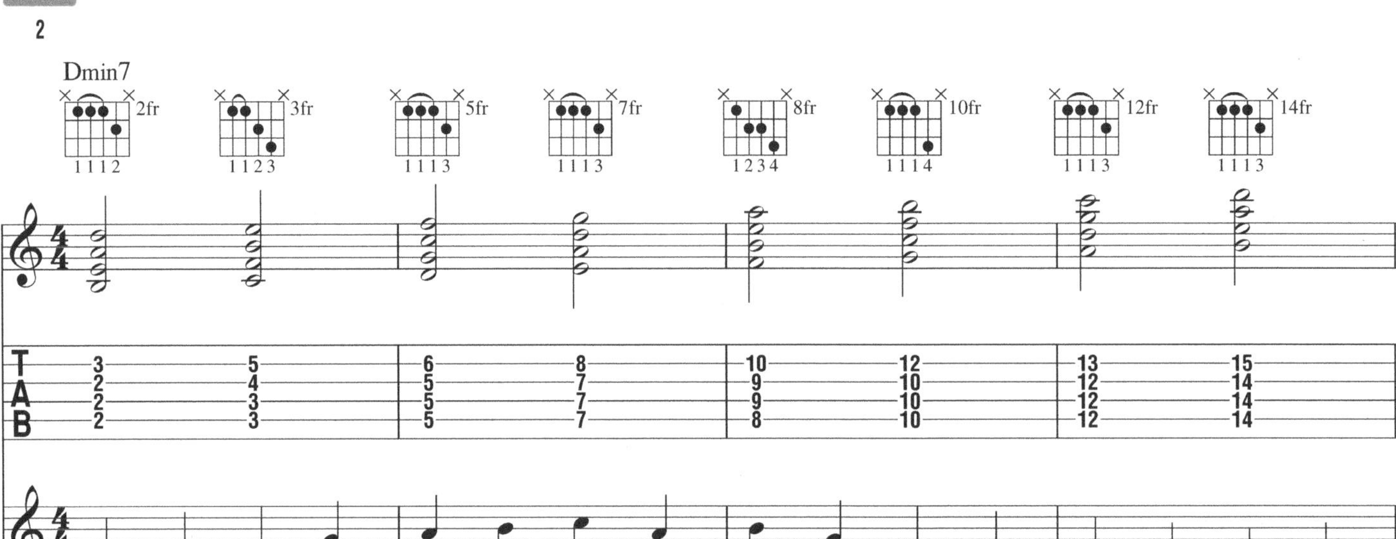

FIG. 2.8. D Dorian Variation with Bass Line

3

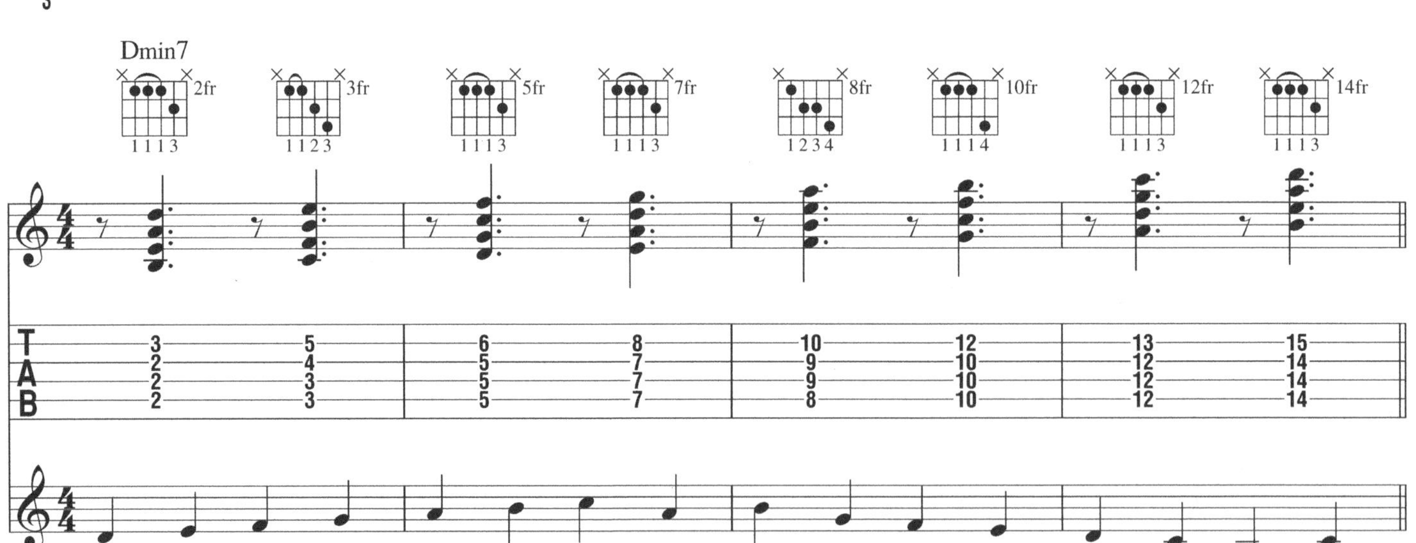

FIG. 2.9. D Dorian Variation on "And" of 1

Chordal players take their choice from any of the eight eighth-notes found in each bar. You may choose to play on beats 1, 2, 3, 4, or the "up beats" of each. You may vary the number of attacks per bar, but it's easiest to start with one. Here is a set of choices using only one attack per measure.

4

Dmin7

2fr (1 1 1 3)	3fr (1 1 2 3)	5fr (1 1 1 3)	7fr (1 1 1 3)
3 2 2 2	5 4 3 3	6 5 5 5	8 7 7 7

8fr (1 2 3 4)	10fr (1 1 1 4)	12fr (1 1 1 3)	14fr (1 1 1 3)
10 9 9 8	12 10 10 10	13 12 12 12	15 14 14 14

FIG. 2.10. D Dorian Variation on "And" of 2

5

Dmin7
2fr
3fr
5fr
7fr
9fr
10fr
12fr

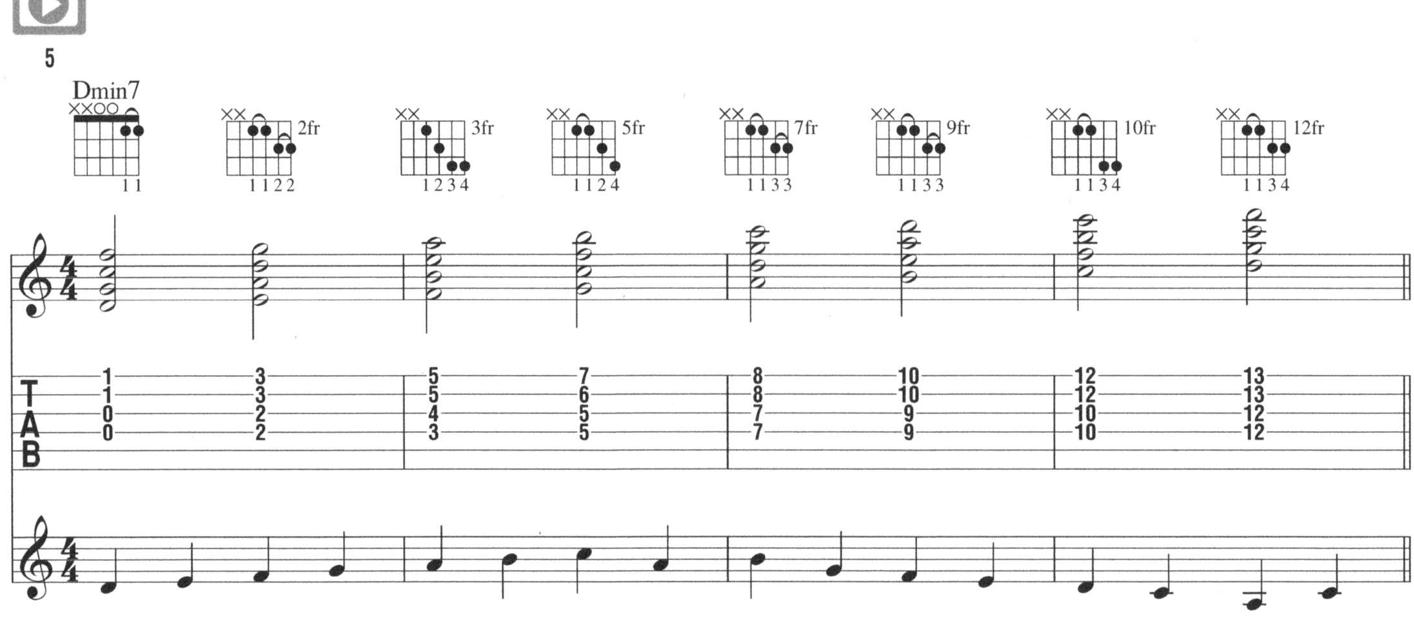

FIG. 2.11. D Dorian Variation on Top Four Strings

6

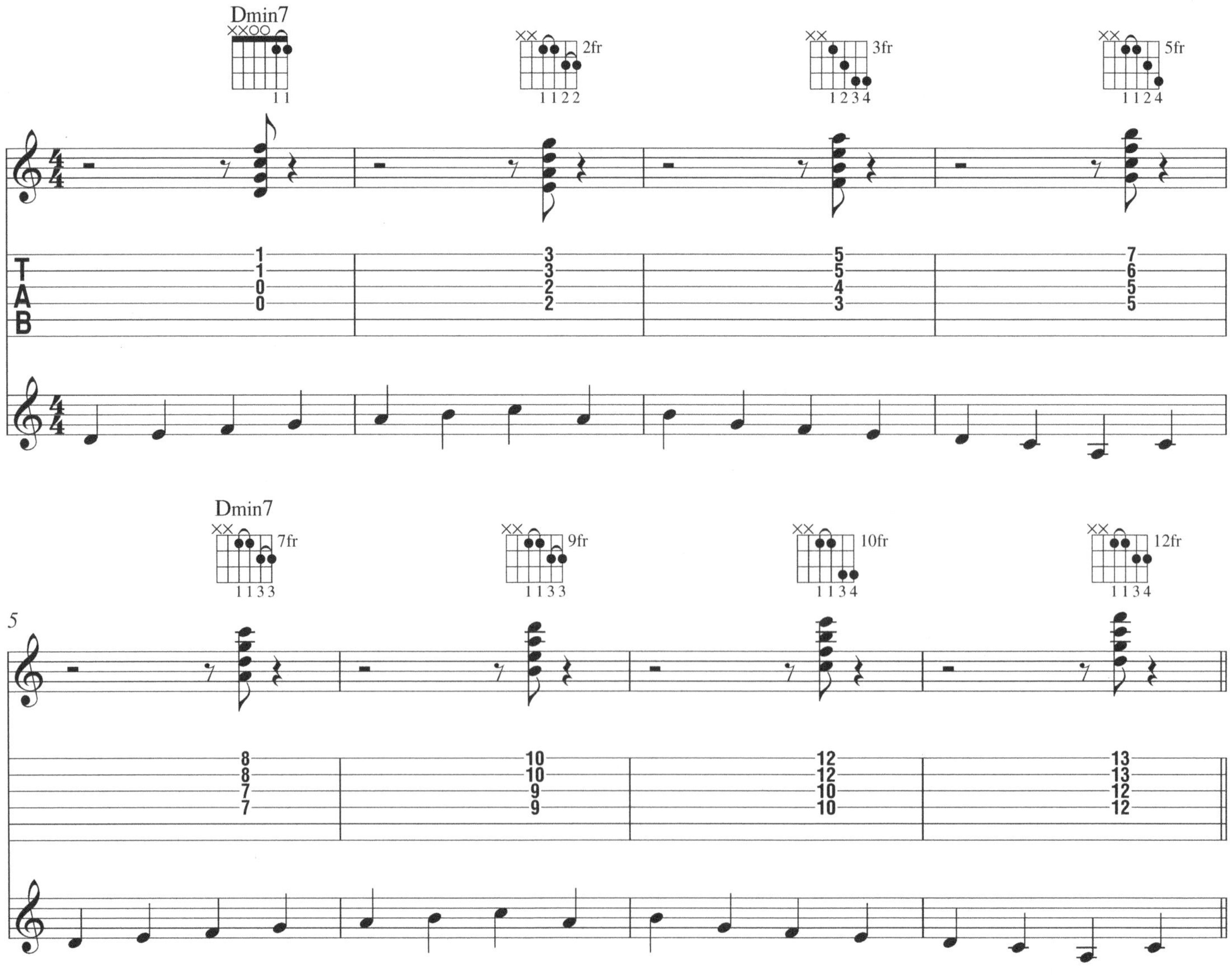

Dmin7
2fr
3fr
5fr
Dmin7
7fr
9fr
10fr
12fr

FIG. 2.12. D Dorian Variation on the "And" of Beat 3

Here, we are mixing up the top two string sets.

7

FIG. 2.13. D Dorian Variation Mixing Top String Sets

For another variation, let's try the "and" of beat 1, using both long and short note values.

8

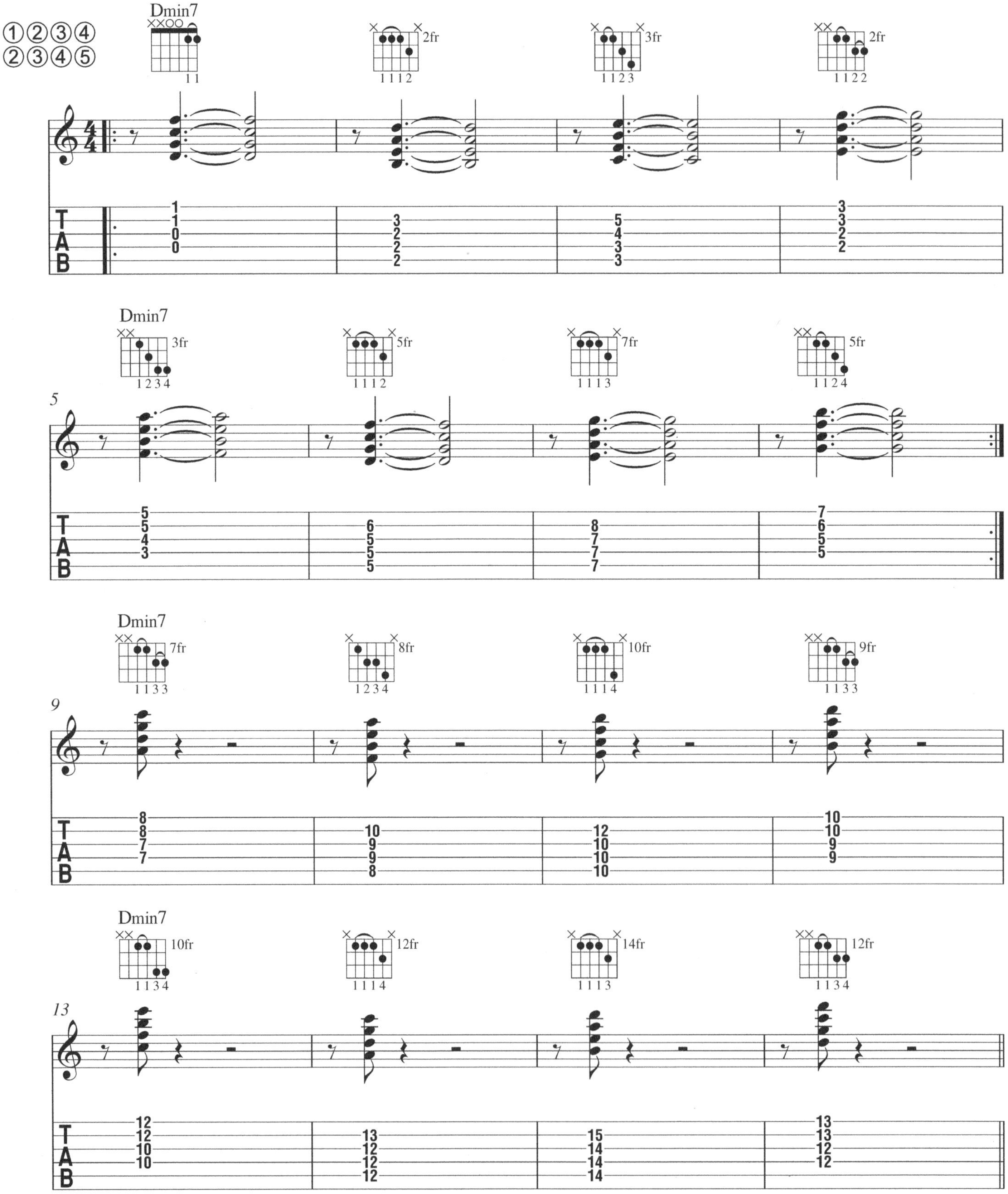

①②③④
②③④⑤

Dmin7

Dmin7

Dmin7

Dmin7

FIG. 2.14. Mixing Top String Sets on "And" of 1

CHAPTER 3

Tension and Release through Choice of Voicing

Musical performance involves control of points of tension and release. The great musician and Berklee educator John LaPorta (1920 to 2004) compared this ebb and flow to that of a beating heart. When contracted, the heart is in a state of tension, followed by the release. You need to have both states to be functioning well; neither tension nor release is better. In modal music, the chordal player needs to provide these moments for the soloist, the rest of the band, and the listener. Some voicings sound stable, while others, by comparison, sound less stable.

Guitarists often prefer to build voicings from the lower strings up, but most listeners hear voicings in terms of the top note, or lead. Chord tones (R, 3, 5, 7) in the lead tend to sound more stable, promoting a feeling of stability, or release, whereas tensions (9, 11, 13) provide a higher degree of tension. Considering D Dorian, the voicings containing the diatonic tritone interval are the most unstable.

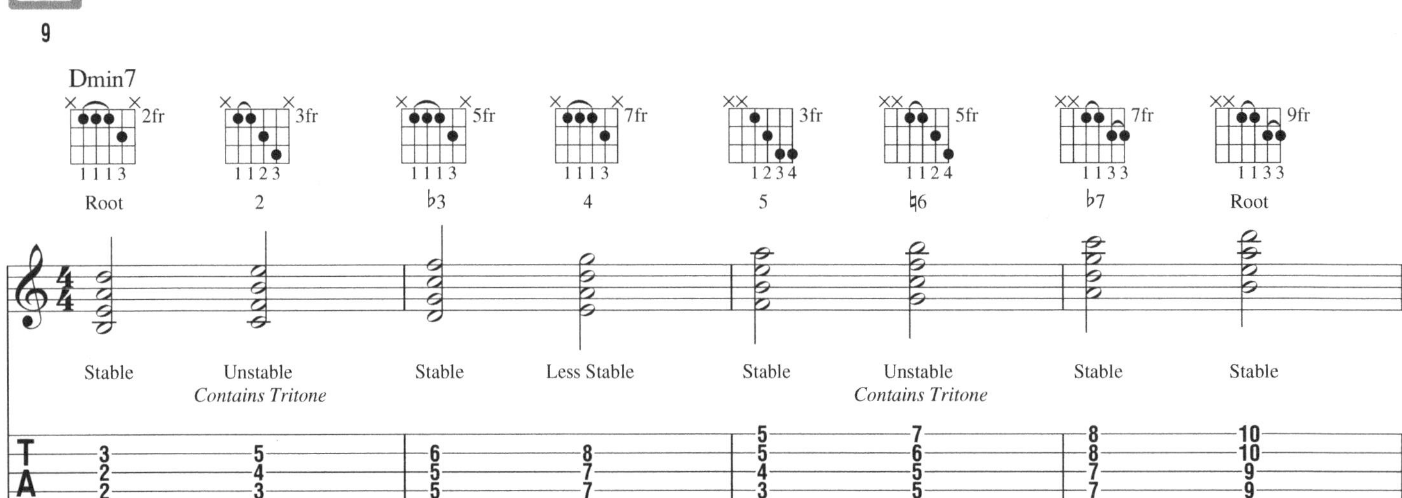

FIG. 3.1. D Dorian Voicings, Comparing Levels of Stability

The double bars found at formal sections are a great point to play the most stable sounds available, enabling a strong sense of release. When playing the progression from "So What" or "Impressions," consider playing a voicing with R, ♭3, 5, ♭7 on top at the double bars at the points found at the formal sections marked AABA. Remember the claps and snaps exercise in chapter 1, "Reinforcing Form through Chordal Accompaniment."

CHAPTER 4

Minor 6 Pentatonic as a Lead Line Harmonized with Dorian

Another way to play modally involves an interesting use of a five-note pentatonic lead line, with that melodic line harmonized with a seven-note scale. This enables guitarists to leap around the given tonality much more freely and unpredictably with harmonically rich textures.

Here are the notes of D minor 6 pentatonic. This scale functions the same as D Dorian, but it contains only five notes (2 and ♭7 are omitted).

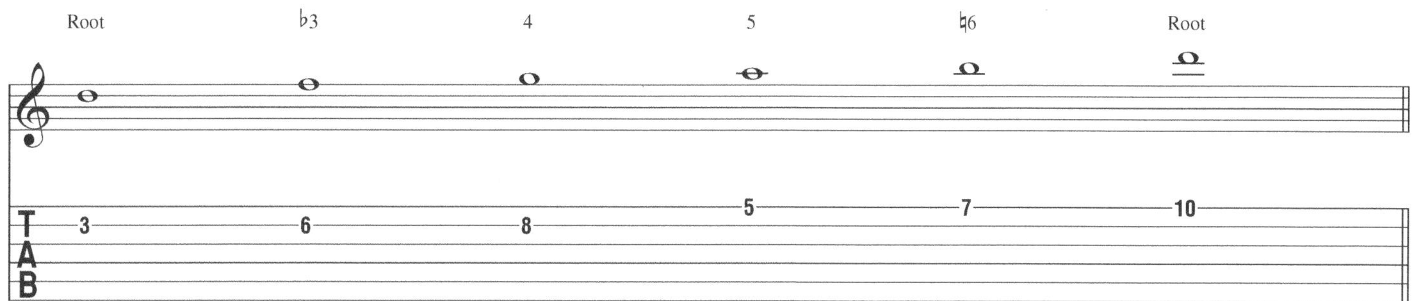

FIG. 4.1. Dmin6 Pentatonic

In the following example, you'll see the five notes of Dmin6 pentatonic harmonized with all seven notes of D Dorian. (The 2 and ♭7 are found in the voicings.)

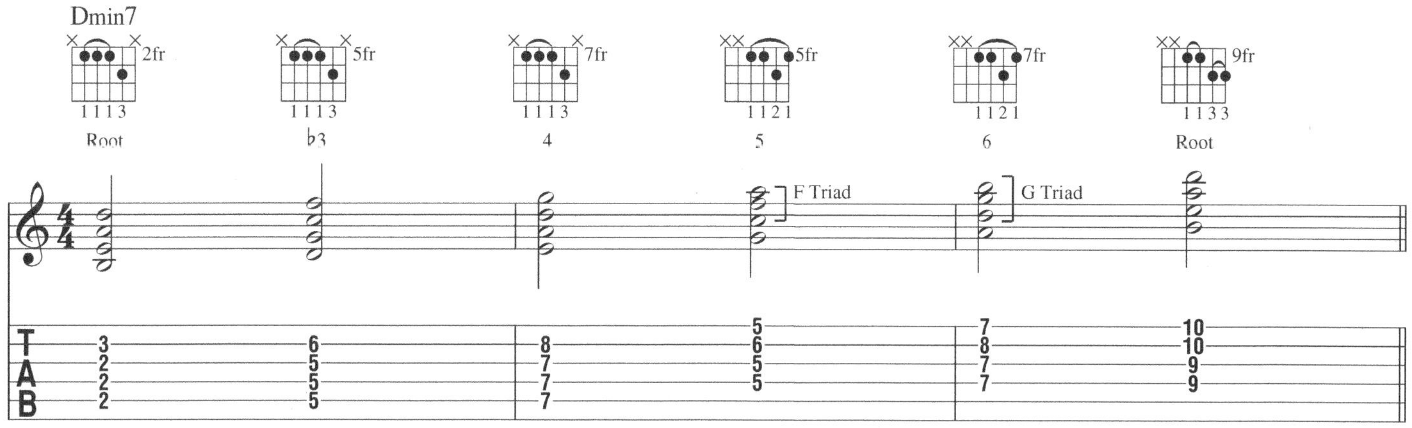

FIG. 4.2. Dmin6 Pentatonic and D Dorian

You'll notice that the sounds don't strictly consist of fourth intervals—in fact, there are major triads built on F and G where the 5th and 6th degrees are in the melody. You might wonder why these voicings are included in a section dealing with quartal harmony. As it turns out, they serve as a variation of a voicing that involves five notes, all a fourth below the lead. The A in the melody comes from inversion of the note found three perfect fourths below the F in the lead.

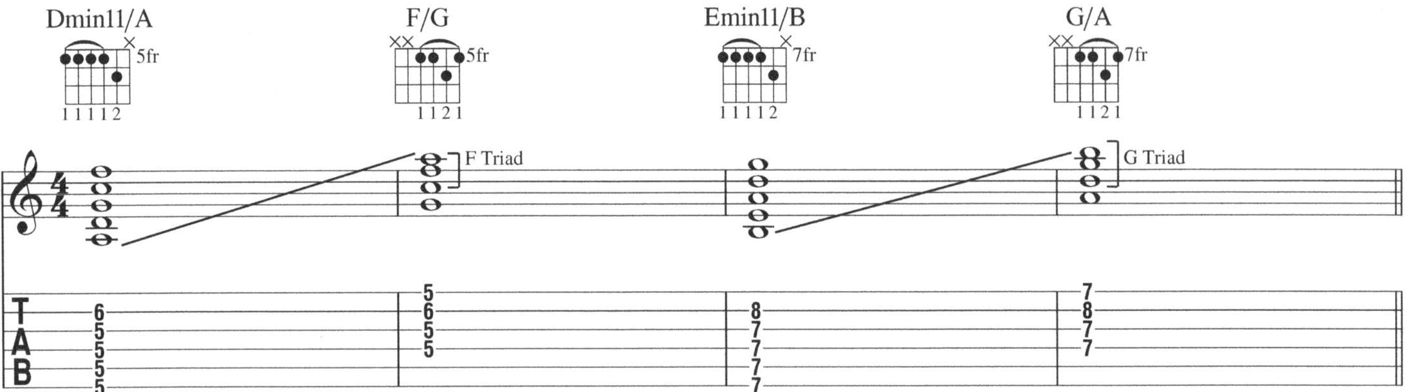

FIG. 4.3. D Dorian Variation with Five Notes

These two voicings can be seen as F/G and G/A or more commonly as "So What" voicings, since these voicings are a very close simplification found in the landmark recording on Miles Davis' *Kind of Blue* and similar works.

Work to integrate these shapes into your repertoire. These sounds will serve you well for D Dorian and, as we'll soon see, G Mixolydian too.

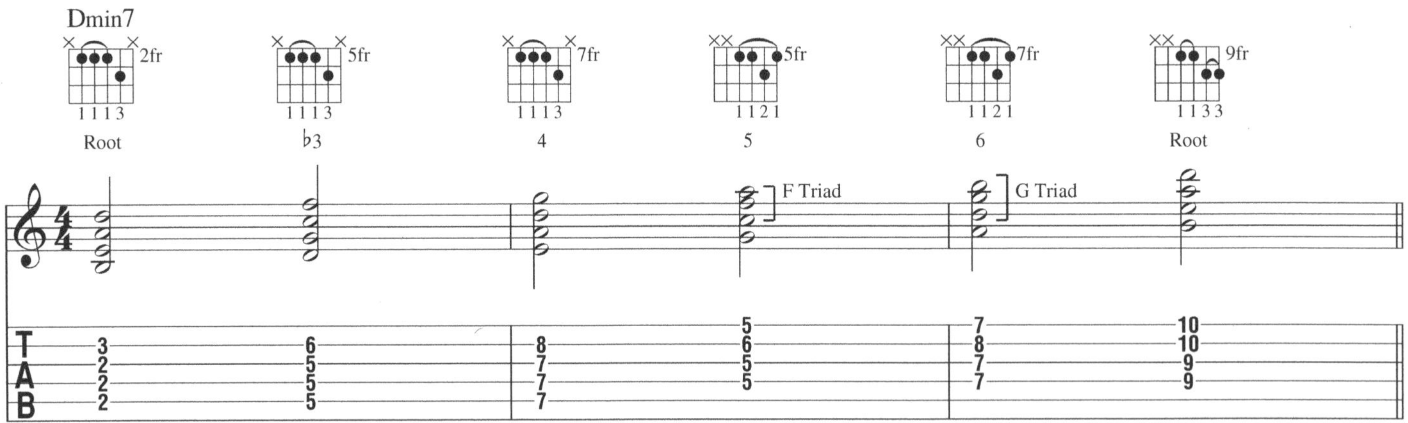

FIG. 4.4. Dmin6 Pentatonic and D Dorian

Seen another way, graphically on a fretboard:

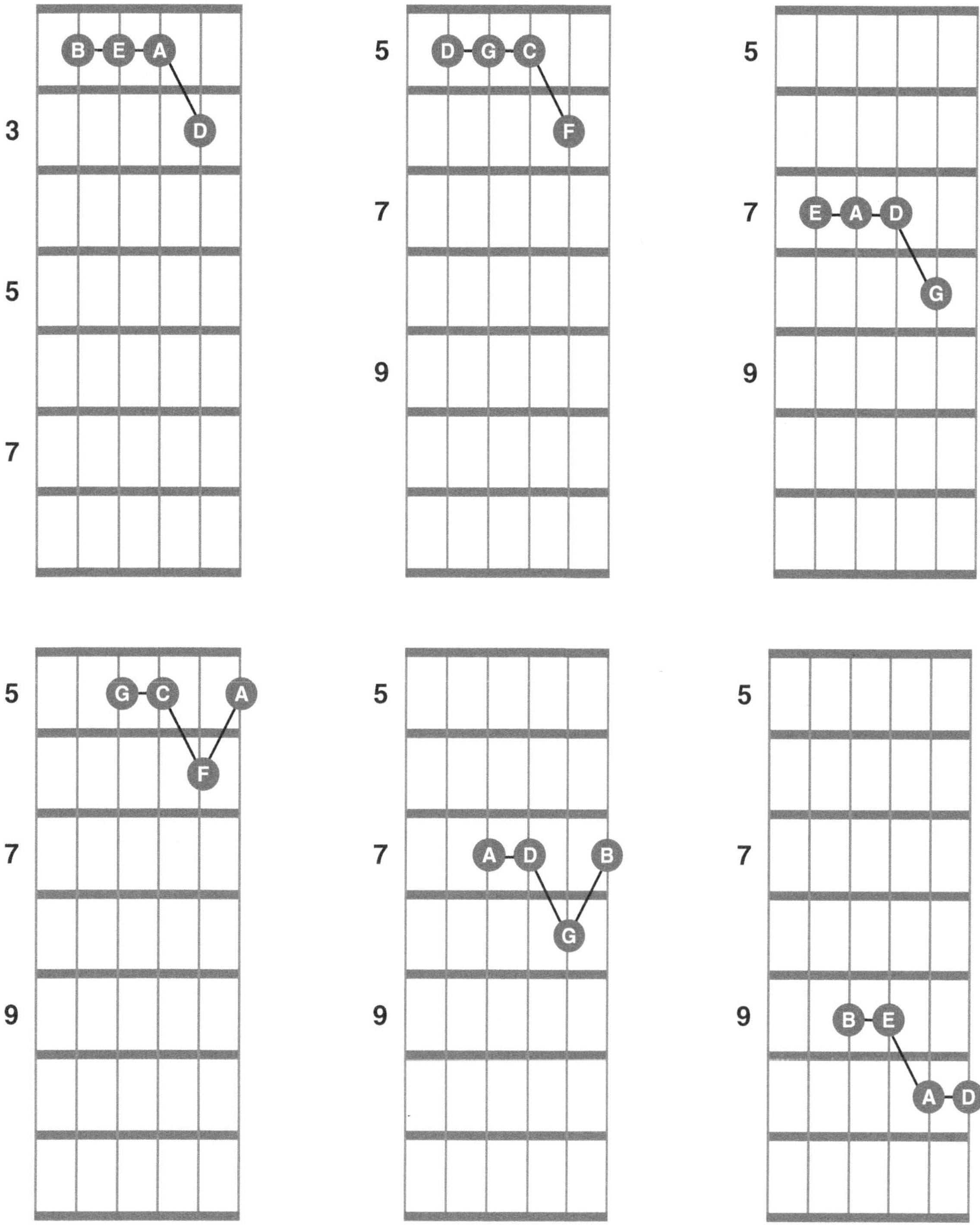

FIG. 4.5. D Minor 6 Lead Line, D Dorian Harmony Fretboard Diagrams

CHAPTER 5

Chordal Embellishments Using Chromatic and Diatonic Material

Another way to create tension and release in guitar voicings is to start with a single shape, and hold the top note as a pedal point. It's possible to use the technique of "planing" chromatically or diatonically, with respect to a pedal point on top to achieve an interesting effect. "Planing" refers to making use of notes in adjacent parallel structures—exploring a parallel "plane." The term "side slipping" is sometimes used for this approach. Tension is created by the resultant chromaticism. Release is achieved by returning to the original voicing.

Let's do chromatic planing first. Starting from the F/G shape, keep the top note the same and move the bottom three notes in parallel. The notes are chromatically planing around the original voicing. It's necessary to rearrange your fretting fingers a bit, but the resulting sounds are very impressive, especially considering the small amount of work you need to do.

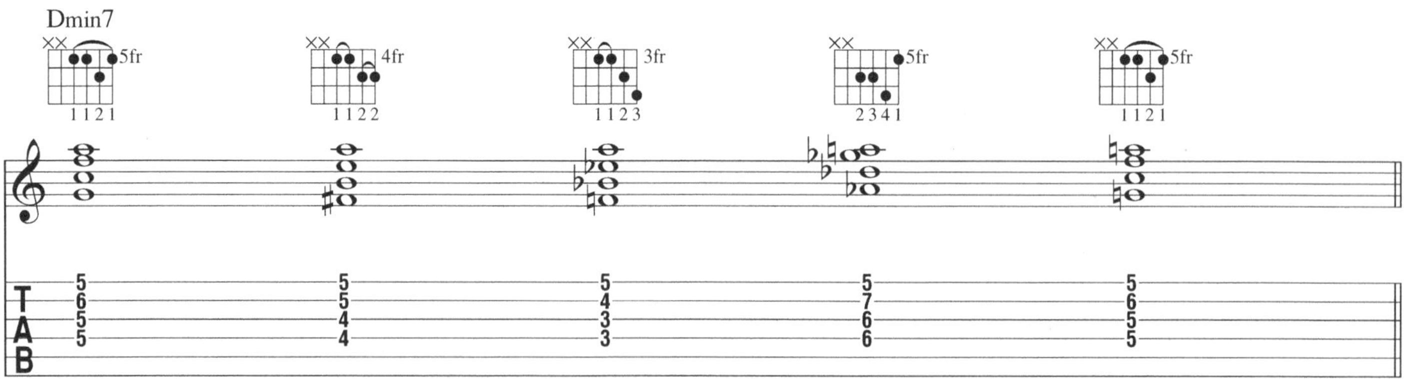

FIG. 5.1. Chromatic Planing with Pedal Point in Top Line

It's possible to use this technique starting with each of the minor 6 pentatonic lead note voicings as a source. When experimenting with this concept, it's best to avoid producing octaves; the tension needs to contain four different notes, and an octave spoils the effect. Here's a set of possibilities, all based on D minor.

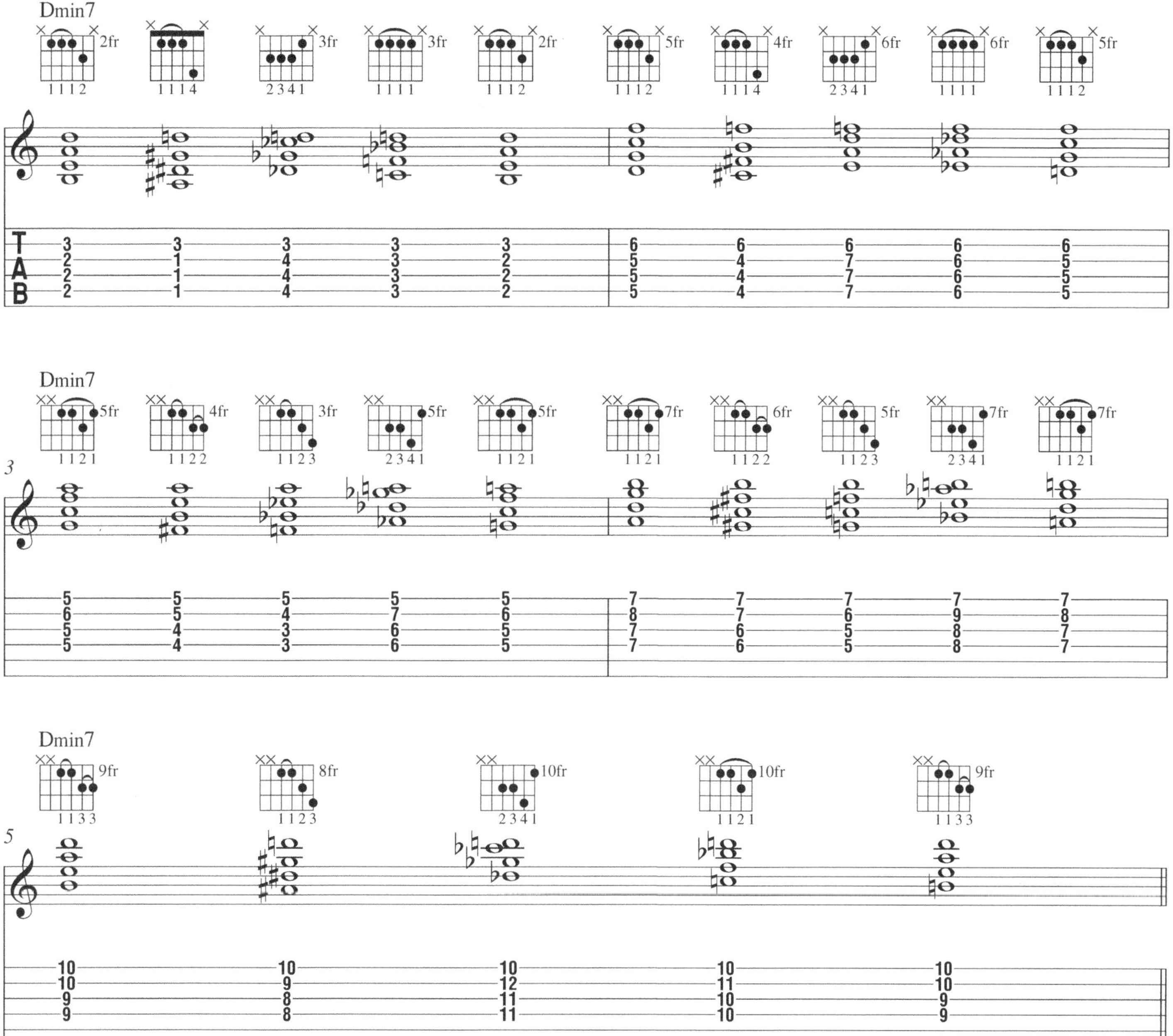

FIG. 5.2. D Minor Chromatic Planing with Pedal Point in Top Line

Diatonic planing with respect to a pedal point in the top voice involves diatonic motion of voices. Starting with each of the voicings with Dmin6 pentatonic as a lead line will give you some more attractive options for comping.

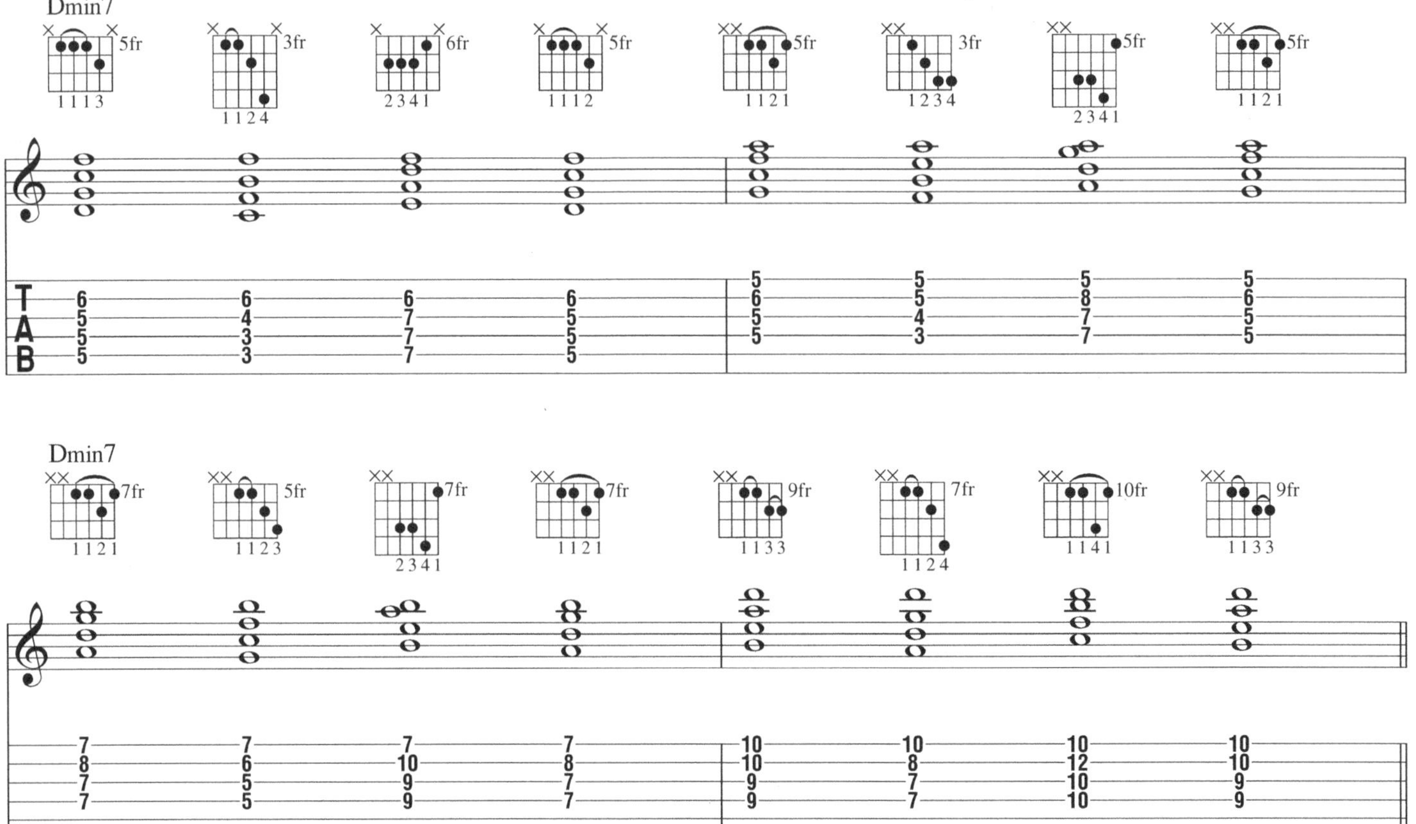

FIG. 5.3. Dmin6 Voicings

Practice voicings using D Dorian, Dmin6 pentatonic, chromatic, and diatonic playing.

3, 4

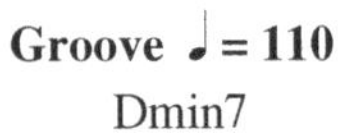

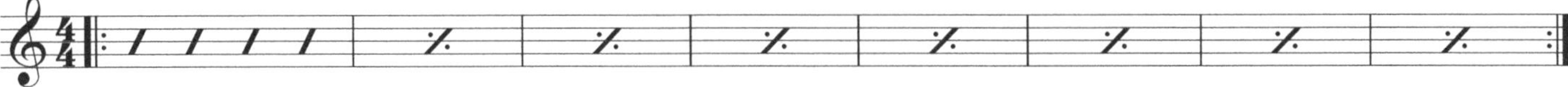

FIG. 5.4. D Minor Groove

CHAPTER 6

Quartal Voicings on the "So What/Impressions" Progression

Bill Evans' style of quartal piano voicings, similar to what he used on "So What," from Miles Davis' classic album *Kind of Blue,* can be played on the guitar in simplified form as follows. A sections are in D minor, B sections are up a half-step, in E♭ minor. Play through the progression.

FIG. 6.1. Bill Evans "So What" Simplified Voicings

Four years later, in 1963, John Coltrane recorded "Impressions," a composition based on the same progression. McCoy Tyner played voicings similar to the following, adapted for the guitar.

A
Dmin7 Amin/B G/A

B
E♭min7 B♭min/C A♭/B♭

A
Dmin7 Amin/B G/A

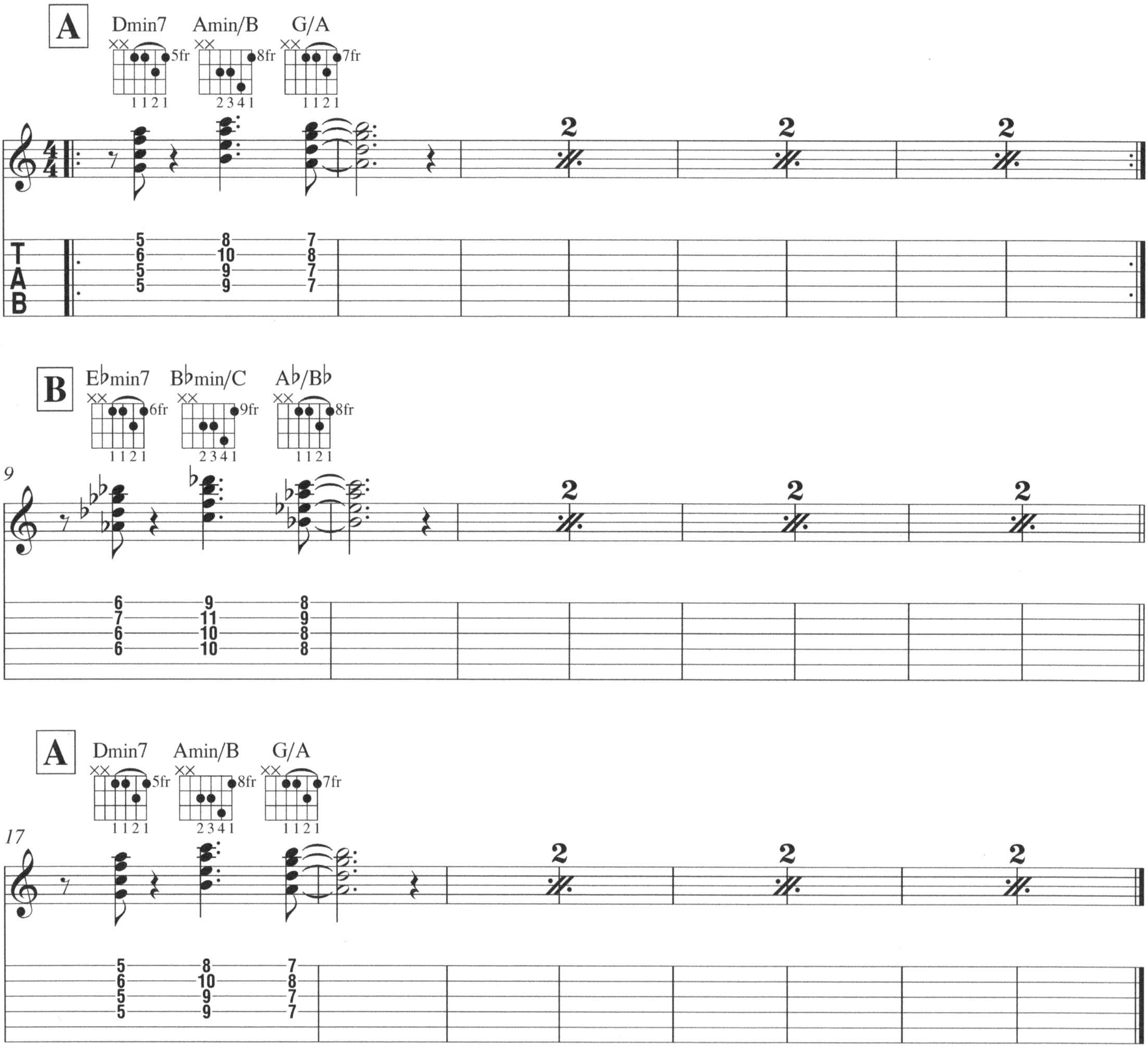

FIG. 6.2. McCoy Tyner "Impressions" Simplified Voicings

"Impressions" can be seen as a more aggressive, modified update to "So What," in part due to its quicker tempo and increased interaction with the rhythm section. Regarding the chords played during the melody, we also see increased energy. Instead of two attacks in each phrase, as found in "So What," we find three attacks. In "Impressions," the "So What" voicings are found in reverse order with a dissonant voicing inserted between them. The second voicing in the sequence, notated here as Amin7/B contains a flat-9 interval between the bottom note (B) and the top note (C), adding a higher degree of tension, setting the stage for a dramatic release.

Modal playing involves skilled control of tension and release, most often with clear statements at the double bars, found in every eight bars.

On the live recording of *Impressions*, pianist McCoy Tyner stops playing at about 2:30, leaving John Coltrane on tenor saxophone, Jimmy Garrison on acoustic bass, and Elvin Jones on drums. Released decades later, in 2018, a Coltrane album *Both Directions at Once* contains several takes of "Impressions," including Takes 3 and 4, both with no piano accompaniment. I recommend that you play and overdub chordal accompaniment as a practicing technique. Playing along with great recordings is a productive and fun way to develop experience, facility, vocabulary, and endurance. Using your recording software to overdub your own chordal accompaniment provides a very efficient method for improvement. Listening back to your recorded comping is the fastest way to notice (1) what sounds good, (2) what still needs work, and (3) what to do about it. For further practice, see appendix A for a comprehensive list of "Great 'Pianoless Trio' Jazz Recordings for Practicing Chordal Accompaniment."

CHAPTER 7

Dorian and Minor 6 Pentatonic over Dominant 7sus Chords

Use of Dorian and minor-6 pentatonic voicings can be very easily adapted for use on dominant seventh chords.

Let's look at the D Dorian voicings that we know and analyze the chord tones with respect to G7. Any extended period (two or more bars) of G7 can be well covered by these voicings.

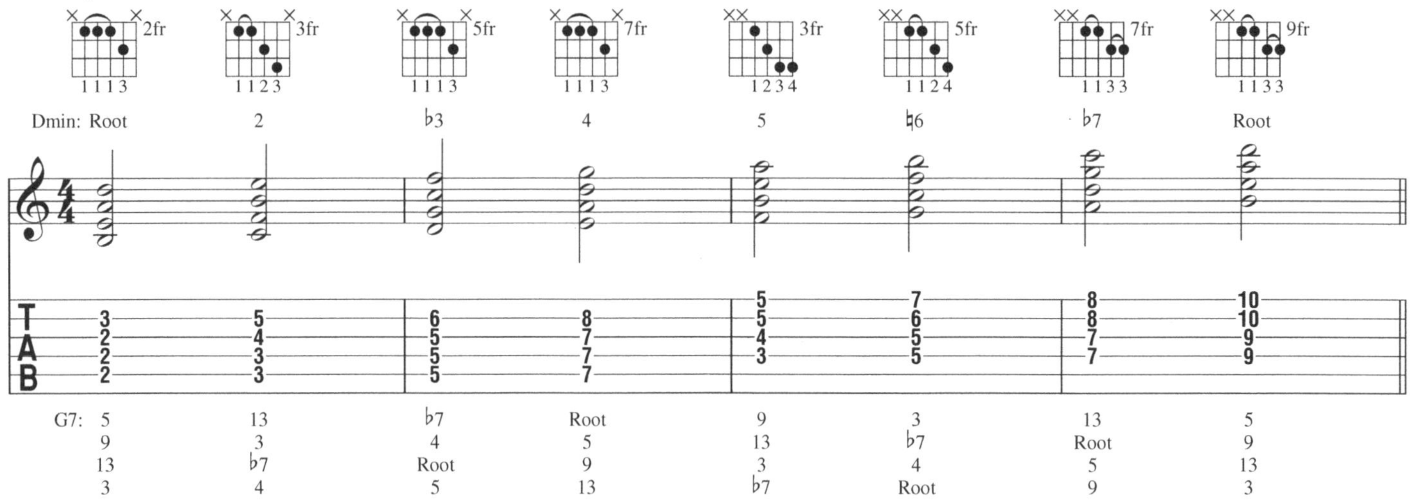

FIG. 7.1. G7 Chord Tones in D Dorian Voicings

The voicing shapes from D minor 6 pentatonic also work as well, or better.

	1	2	3	4	5	6
Position	2fr	5fr	7fr	5fr	7fr	9fr
Fingering	1 1 1 3	1 1 1 3	1 1 1 3	1 1 2 1	1 1 2 1	1 1 3 3
Dmin:	Root	♭3	4	5	6	Root
				F Triad	G Triad	
TAB	3 2 2 2	6 5 5 5	8 7 7 7	5 6 5 5	7 8 7 7	10 10 9 9
G7:	5 9 13 3	♭7 4 Root 5	Root 5 9 13	9 ♭7 4 Root	3 Root 5 9	5 9 13 3

FIG. 7.2. G7 Chord Tones in Dmin6 Pentatonic Voicings

Repetition and transposition are the pathways to fluency! Here is an etude to allow you to get fluent with these voicings, using the Dmin7 G7 and transposing the shapes to the Fmin7 B♭7 set. Move the shapes up three frets for the harmonic change.

5, 6

Funky ♩ = 120

Dmin7

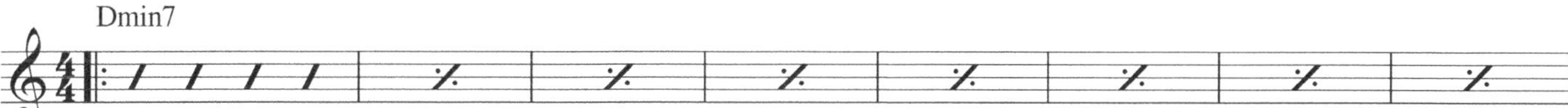

9 G7

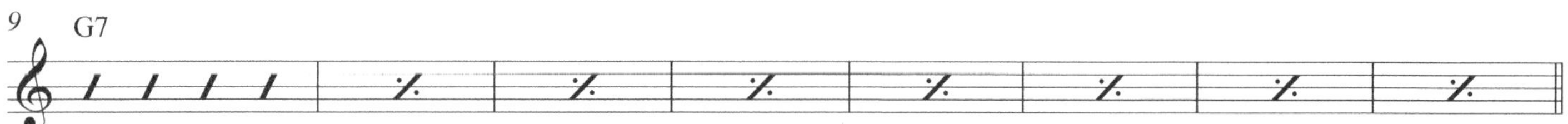

17 Fmin7

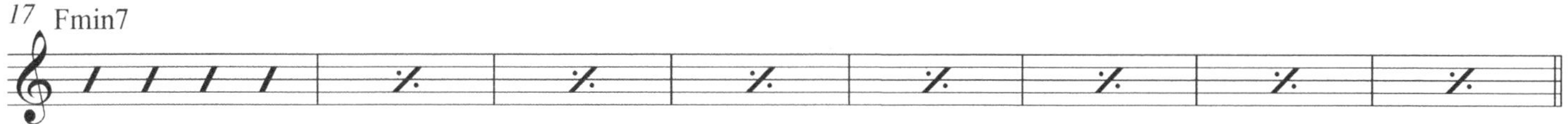

25 B♭7 Dmin7

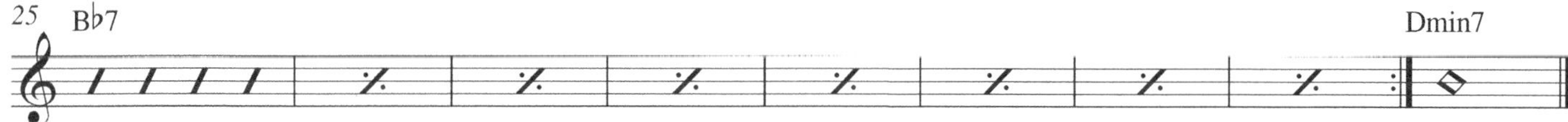

FIG. 7.3. Dmin7 and G7 Voicings Etude

CHAPTER 8

Altered Dominants

The D altered scale, also called D Super Locrian, is a mode found within the E♭ melodic minor scale.

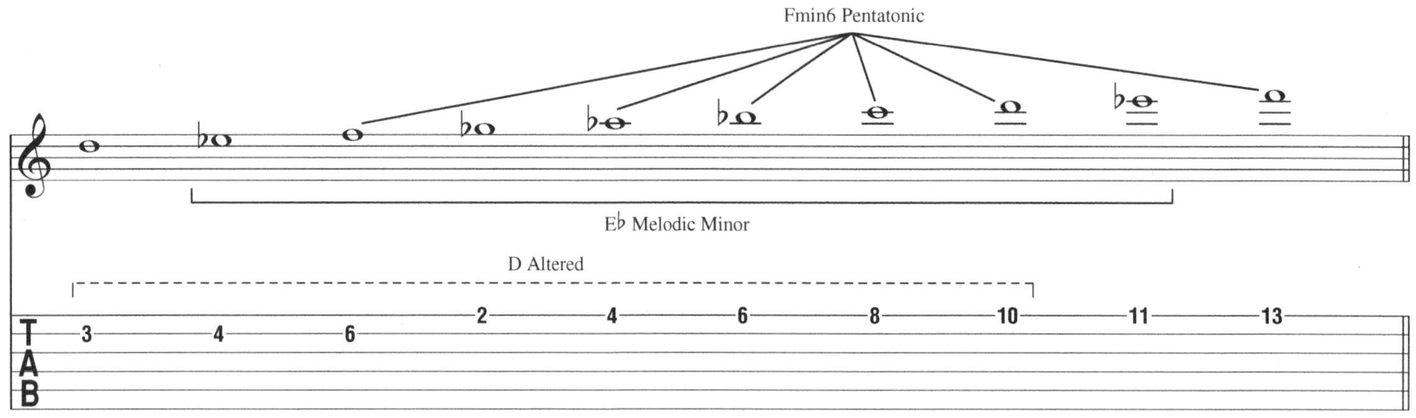

FIG. 8.1. D Altered

There is also a minor 6 pentatonic scale found from F to F in the E♭ melodic minor scale. The minor 6 scale shape is also found from E♭ to E♭ too, but our focus will remain with the F scale.

Looking at D7(alt), the F minor 6 pentatonic scale functions as follows:

FIG. 8.2. Fmin6 Pentatonic Function Over D7(alt)

The five-note F minor 6 pentatonic scale provides a convenient "shortcut" through the seven-note D altered scale sound. Once again, it's useful to use the combination of a five-note lead line, harmonized with a seven-note scale.

Here are the resultant voicings. D7(alt) with F minor 6 pentatonic as a lead line.

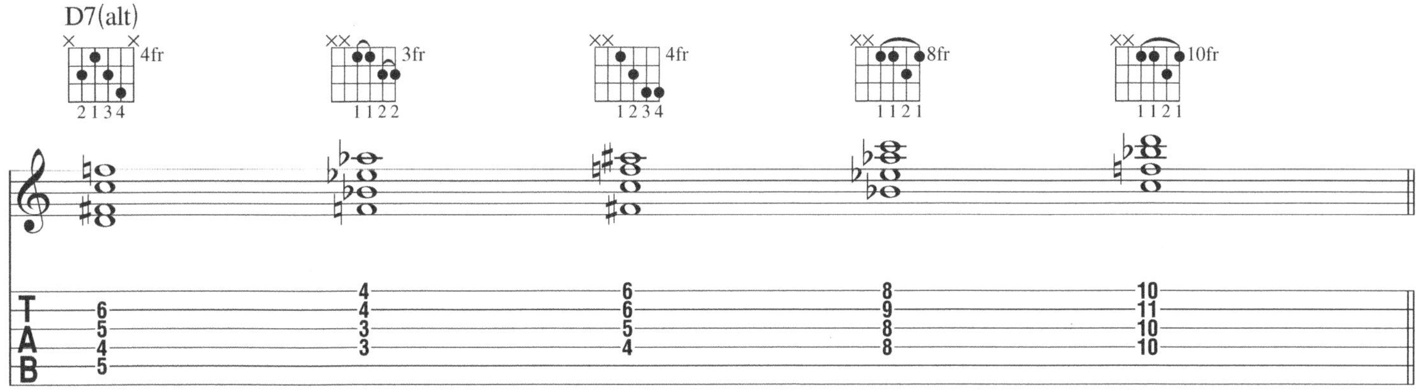

FIG. 8.3. Fmin6 Pentatonic Lead Line Over D7(alt)

Notice the location of the "So What" major triads, appearing with roots on the ♭5 and ♭6 of the dominant chord. It's helpful to make this sort of orientation with the chord of the moment when you're working to superimpose one sound over another.

Here's an etude involving D7(alt) and G7(alt). Work to get a clear sound with each of the voicings while maintaining a musical flow throughout the piece.

7, 8

Spacey Jazz ♩ = 110

D7(alt) G7(alt) F/B♭

FIG. 8.4. D7(alt) and G7(alt) Etude

CHAPTER 9

Quartal Voicings on II V I and G Blues Progressions

QUARTAL VOICINGS ON II V I

Let's look at a way to use quartal/modal sounds in everyday playing situations. When the harmonic rhythm (the speed of chord changes) is moving quickly, chord tones become much more important. When chords are changing quickly, we don't have time to explore the full harmonic landscape, and we need to emphasize chord tones in our voicings. II V I is an extraordinarily common progression, used in many styles. II V I takes us on a quick trip through subdominant, dominant, and tonic functions, and careful choice of quartal/"So What" voicings can blend the modern sound of modal playing while paying respect to proper chord function.

The 3 and 7 are the foundational notes of any chord type beyond a triad. I call the 3 and 7 the "molecules" of chords. The term "molecule" can be defined as the smallest part of a substance that acts like that substance. Elegance involves clever use of the fewest necessary materials. So, when I'm working with students, I suggest that they practice comping through a progression with the root of the chord on the sixth or fifth string, played along with 3/7 or 7/3 on the fourth and third strings. It's important for any guitarist to be able to do this, as every guitarist from Freddie Greene to Steve Cropper to Kurt Rosenwinkel has made use of this approach.

With the modal approach, we're going to have to allow for "incomplete voicings," meaning voicings that imply the chord sound without containing both the 3 and 7 of the chord. Here is II V I using quartal sounds.

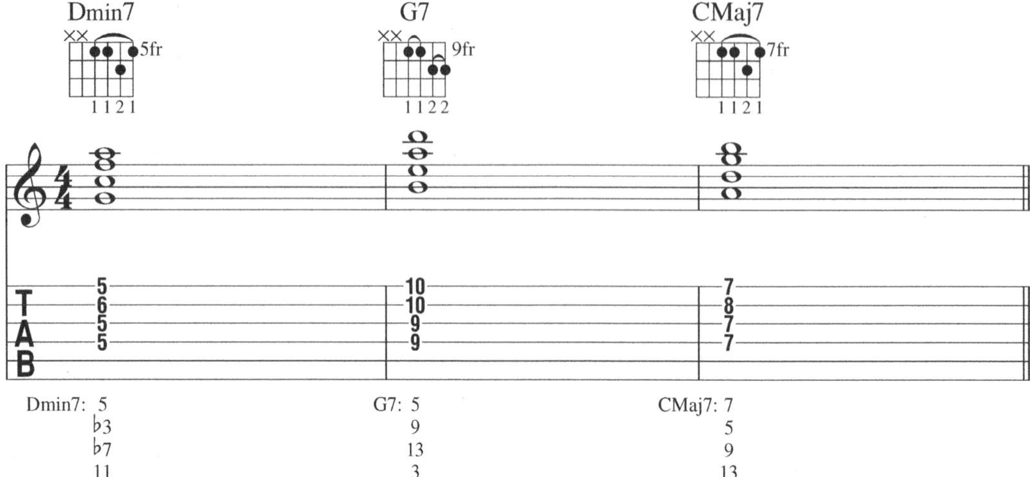

FIG. 9.1. II V I with Quartal Sounds

Note the use of the "So What" major triad shapes along with one purely quartal voicing played in between. The G7 lacks the ♭7 of the chord, but the overall impression of the sequence gets the idea across effectively.

Play through the II V I sequence in twelve keys. Note that it's possible to play the same shapes in several places on the fretboard; the variation presented here is one way that it can be done. Please work to give the chords a balanced sound—no high notes or low notes jumping out louder than their equally important fellow chord tones. Place the chord at the precise rhythmic moment of the chord change for best effect.

9, 10

Latin ♩ = 144

Dmin7 (5fr) G7 (9fr) CMaj7 (7fr) Gmin7 (10fr) C7 (14fr) FMaj7 (12fr)

9

Cmin7 (8fr) F7 (7fr) B♭Maj7 (5fr) Fmin7 (8fr) B♭7 (12fr) E♭Maj7 (10fr)

17

B♭min7 (6fr) E♭7 (5fr) A♭Maj7 (3fr) E♭min7 (11fr) A♭7 (10fr) D♭Maj7 (8fr)

FIG. 9.2. II V I Sequence in Twelve Keys

Here's another variation that you might wish to explore, involving five-note voicings. Note that the dominant chord now has both 3 and 7.

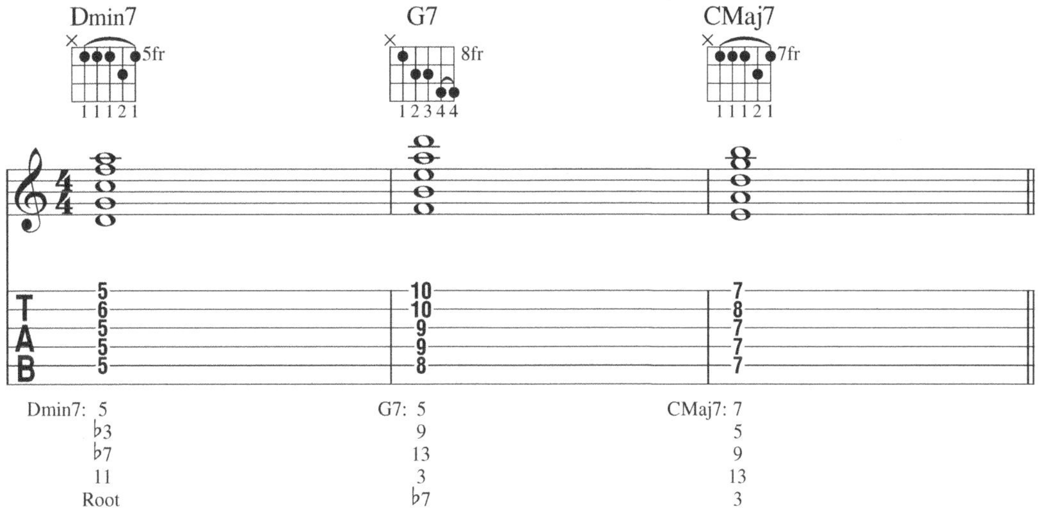

FIG. 9.3. II VI with Five-Note Voicings

Try playing through the previous etude using these five-note voicings to enrich your range of harmonic choices.

QUARTAL VOICINGS ON THE BLUES

Let's apply our set of voicings learned to a G blues progression in 6/4, somewhat similar to the chord progression found on Miles Davis' "All Blues" from the iconic 1959 recording *Kind of Blue*. Here is the progression with the voicing choices we will explore.

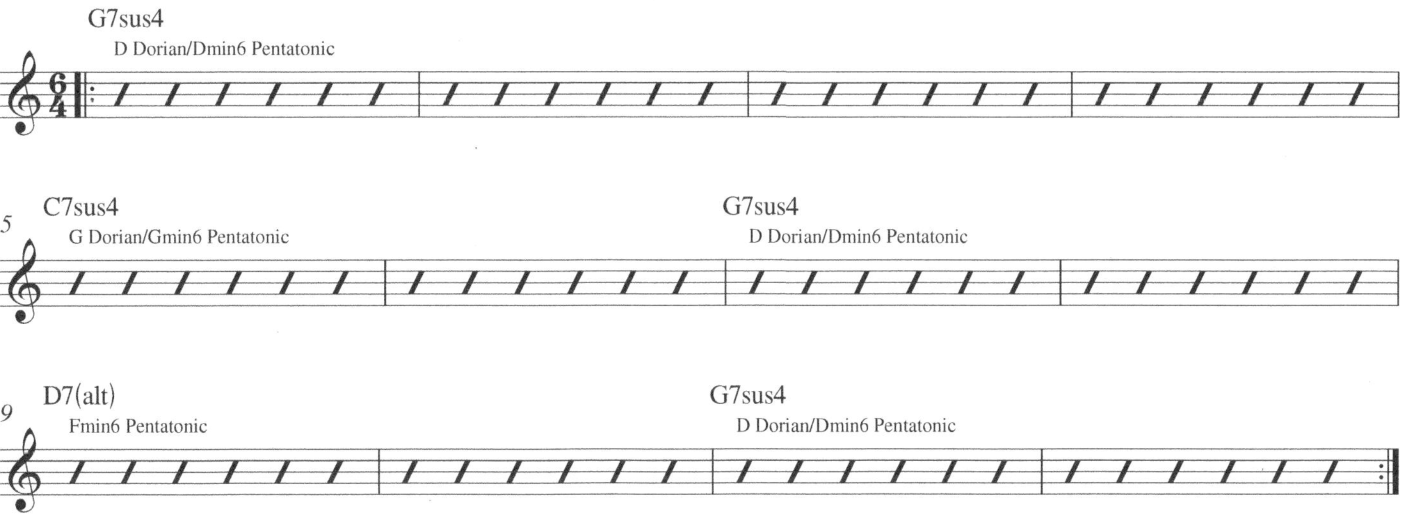

FIG. 9.4. "All Blues" Style Progression

Here's the breakdown.

Chord	Voicings
G7sus4	D Dorian or D minor 6 pentatonic lead line voicings
C7sus4	G Dorian or G minor 6 pentatonic lead line
D7(alt)	F minor 6 pentatonic lead line for D altered scale

10

The C7sus4 requires our use of G Dorian and/or G minor 6 pentatonic lead line voicings. The voicings below work well with extended periods of Gmin7 or C7sus4.

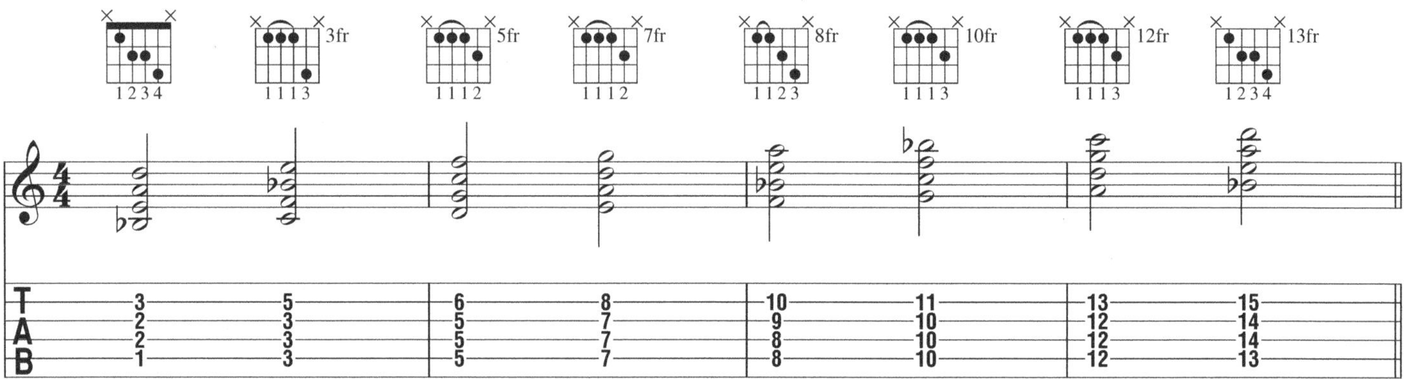

FIG. 9.5. C7 or C7sus for G Dorian Voicings

Here, C7 and/or C7sus are harmonized with the notes from the Gmin6 pentatonic scale. Again, the pentatonic scale melody is enriched by the modal harmony.

11

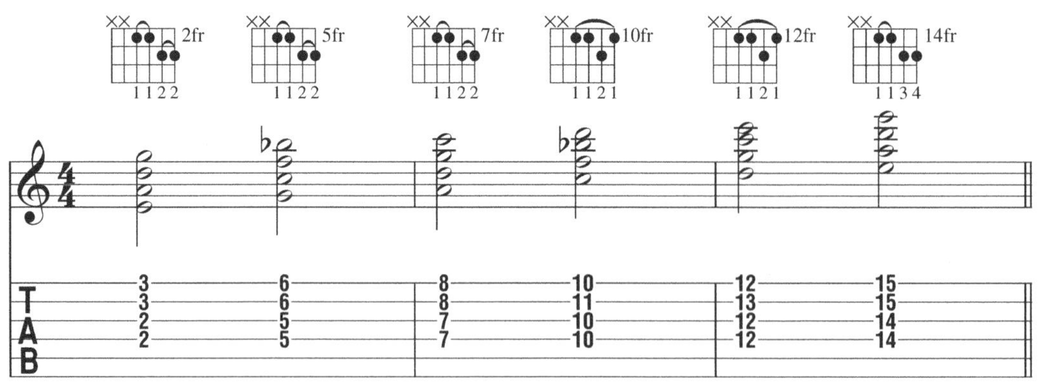

FIG. 9.6. C7 or C7sus4/Gmin6 Pentatonic Melody Harmonized Using G Dorian

G Blues Using Modal Voicings

12

11, 12

Try to play this example both as written as well as loosely interpreted. Also try using the top note as a pedal point with diatonic/chromatic planing (i.e., making use of adjacent chromatic parallel structures).

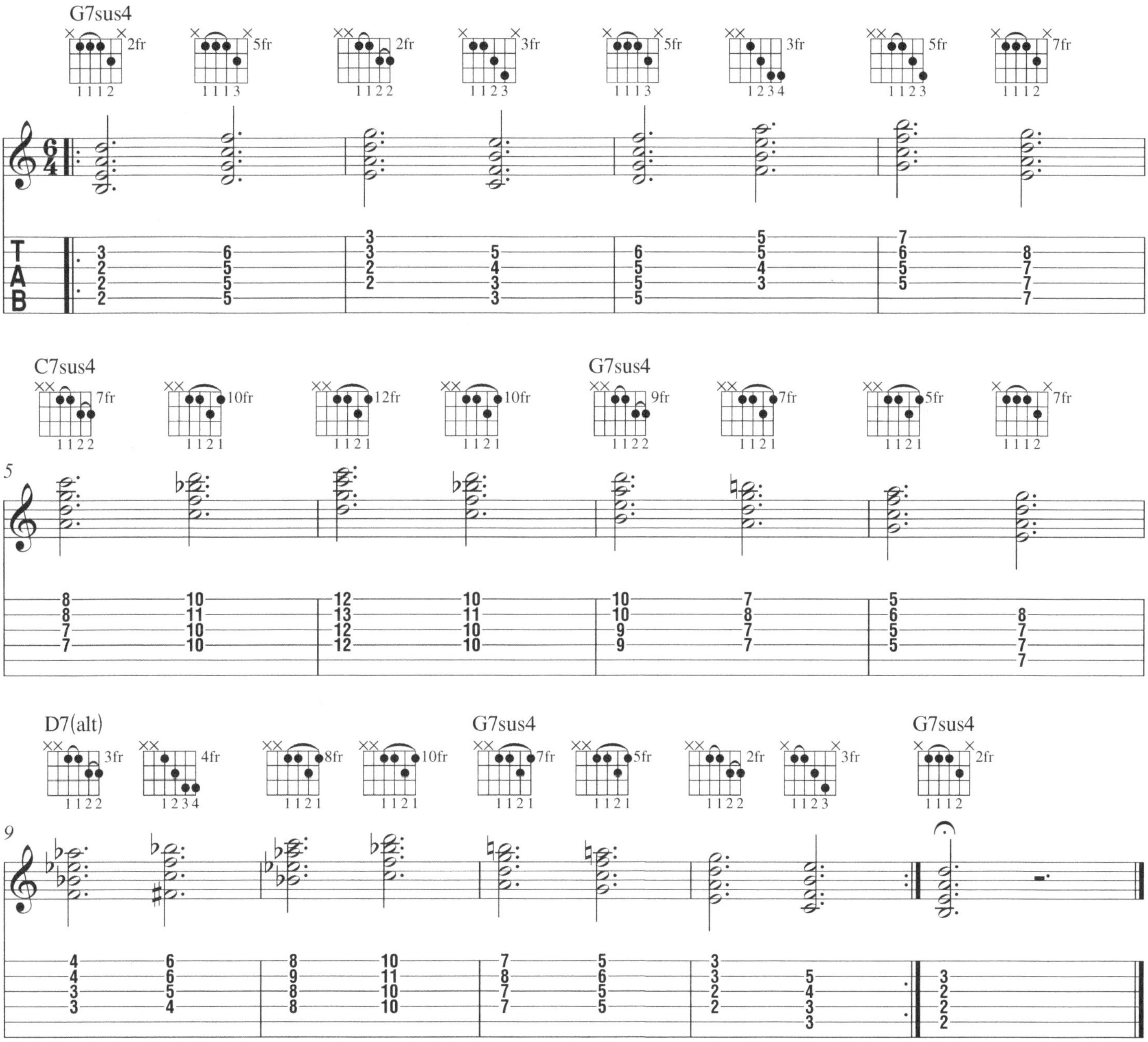

G7sus4

C7sus4 G7sus4

D7(alt) G7sus4 G7sus4

FIG. 9.7. G Blues Using Modal Voicings

13

Here is a transcription of the performance found on the video. The three choruses progress from simpler material to more highly chromatic. Notice the rhythmic choices made throughout, emphasizing the upbeats and use of superimposition of four attacks over six beats for interest and contrast.

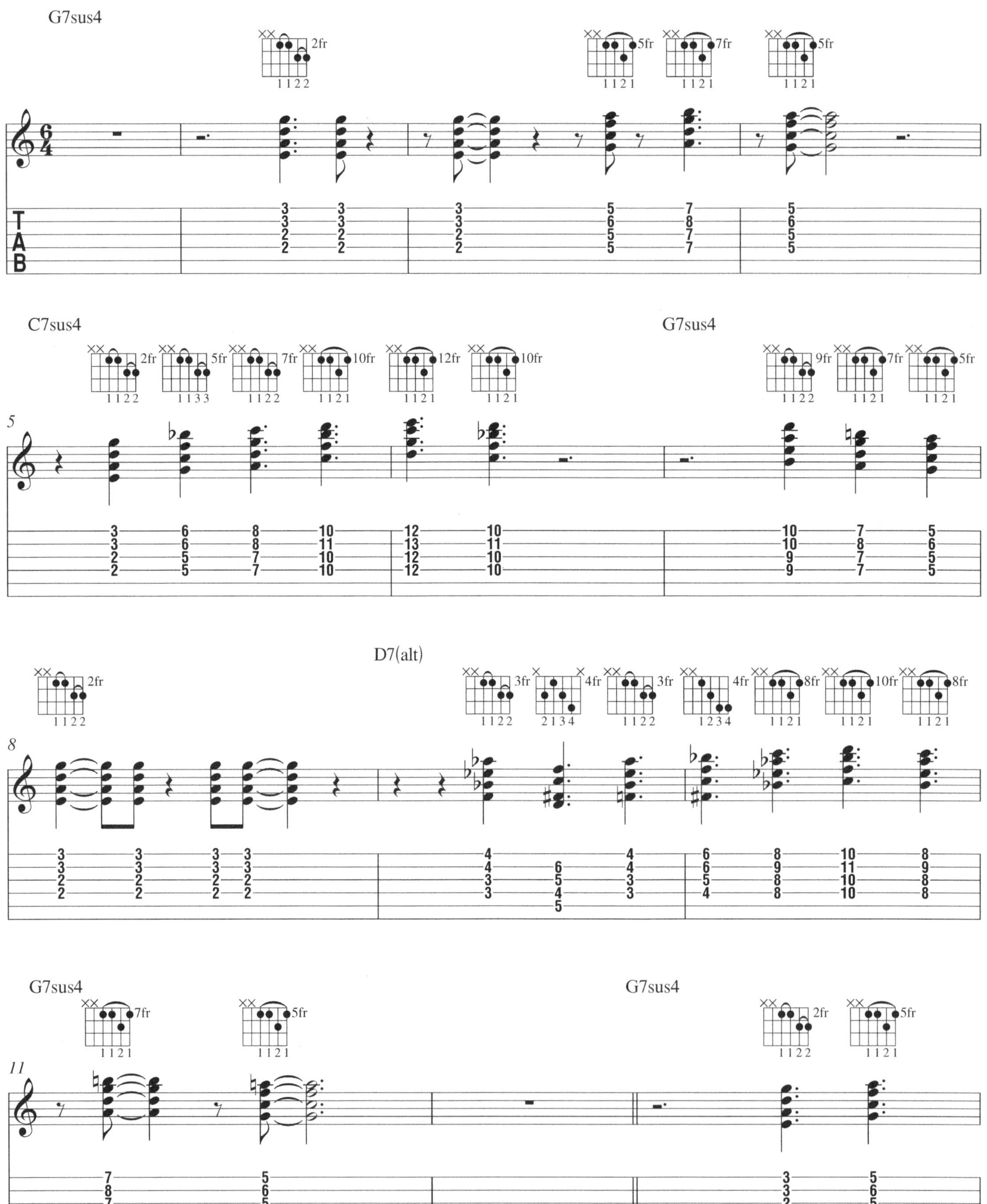
G7sus4
C7sus4
G7sus4
D7(alt)
G7sus4
G7sus4

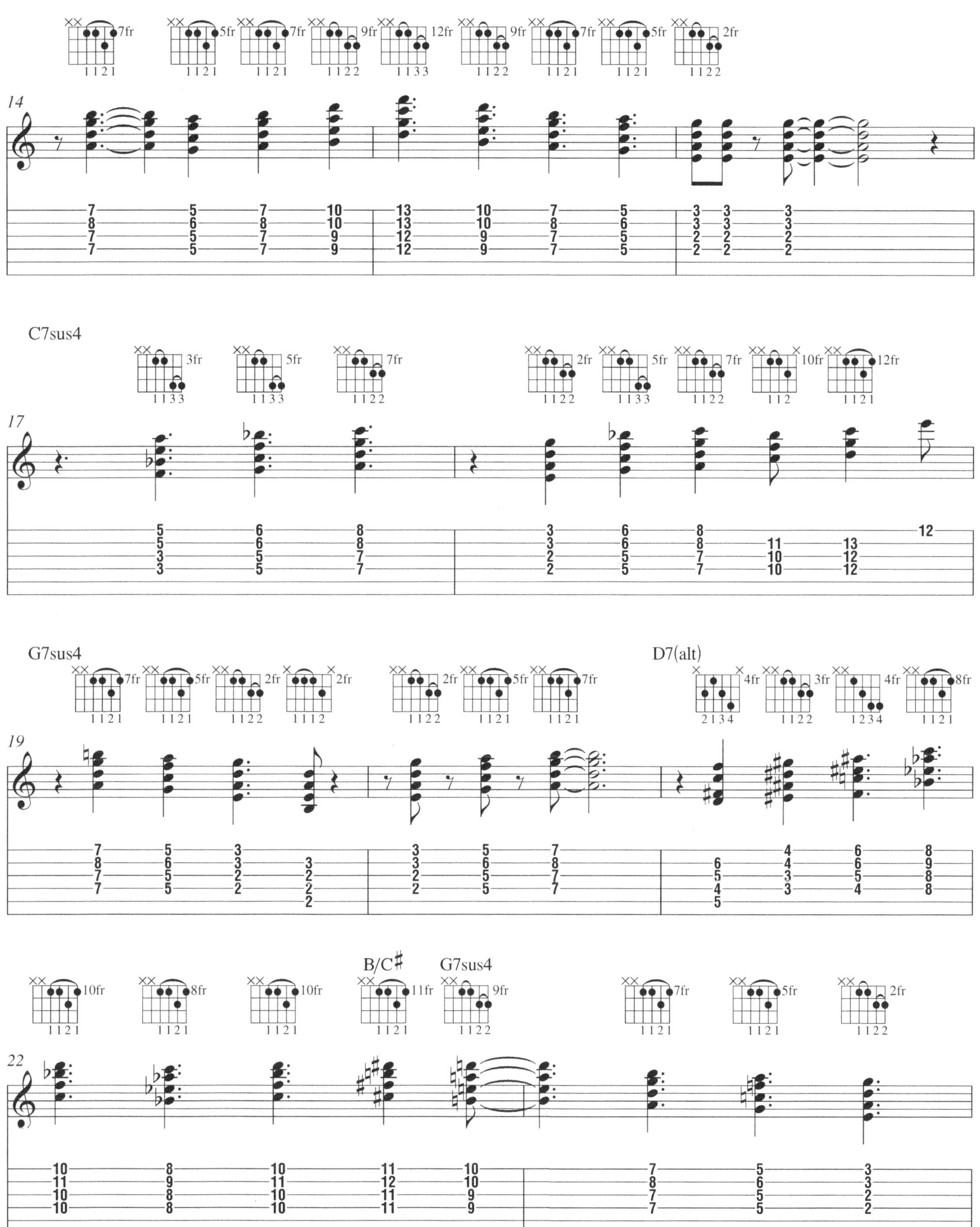
C7sus4
G7sus4
D7(alt)
B/C♯
G7sus4

G7sus4
C7sus4
A♭/B♭
G7sus4

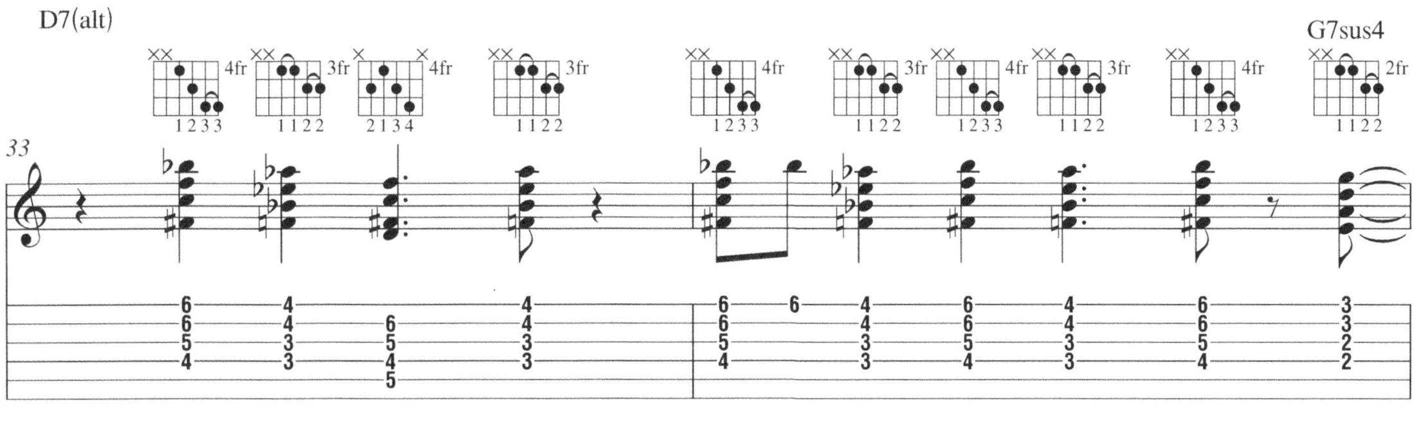

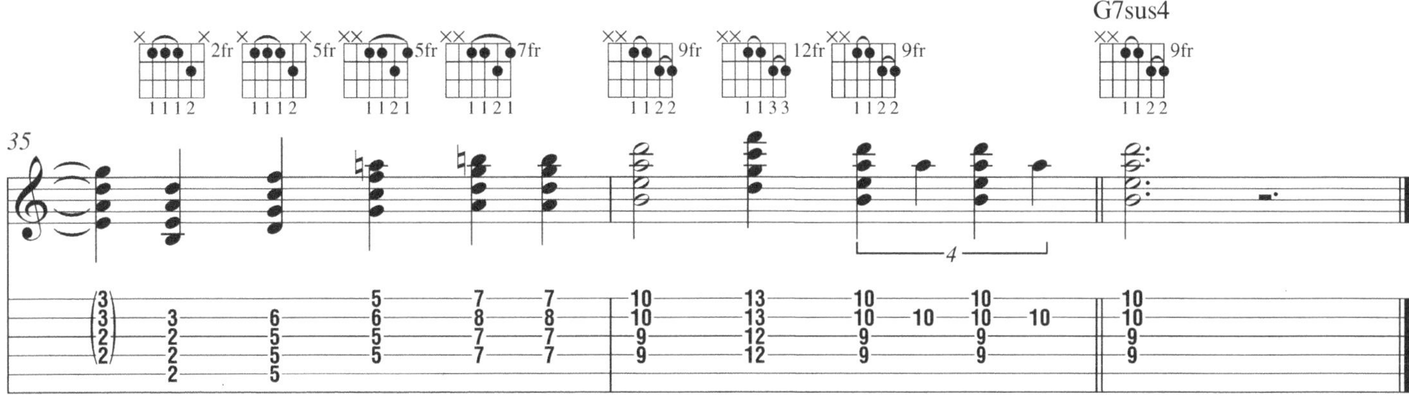

FIG. 9.8. Transcription of G Blues in 6/4

CHAPTER 10

Gospel-Influenced Modal Voicings and the Gospel Scale

Have you ever played this while jamming on a G7?

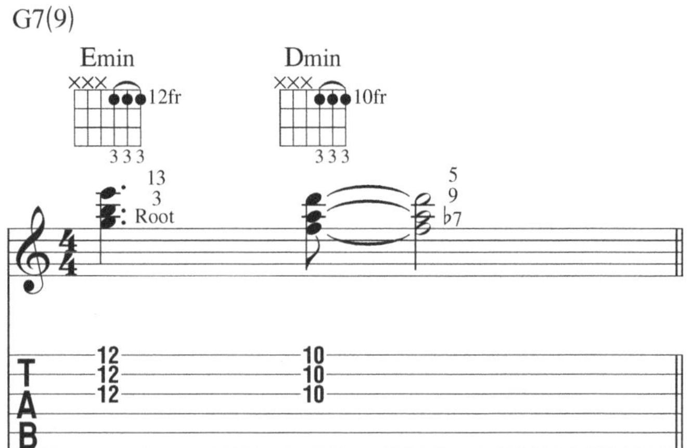

FIG. 10.1. G7(9) Chord Progression

Modal voicings do not necessarily need to be quartal in structure. Guitarists can take liberties on an extended period of dominant seventh harmony through use of triadic sounds.

Running a sequence of two triads, using inversions, can give a feeling of interesting motion. Using a couple of upper-structure triads (USTs) can be a useful device. An upper-structure triad is a triad that contains one or more tensions of a given chord. Thinking in terms of USTs can allow you to get complex sounds by means of using a simple device.

For G7, Emin would be an upper-structure triad, as it contains the T13 (E) as well as the root (G) and 3 (B) of the chord. Dmin would also work well, as the chord tones D, F, and A provide the 5, ♭7, and T9.

Using both of these triads in a chordal sequence yields an interesting splash of color over G7. Think of minor triads built from the 5 and 6 above the root of the dominant seventh chord. The six notes found in these two triads yield six of the seven notes found in G Mixolydian. The only missing note is the avoid note, C.

Dominant 7 Chord	Related Roman Numerals	Triads
G7	VImin and Vmin	Emin Dmin

Many guitarists have used the Emin Dmin pairing shown above, but it's really useful to follow through with the idea, playing through all of the inversions.

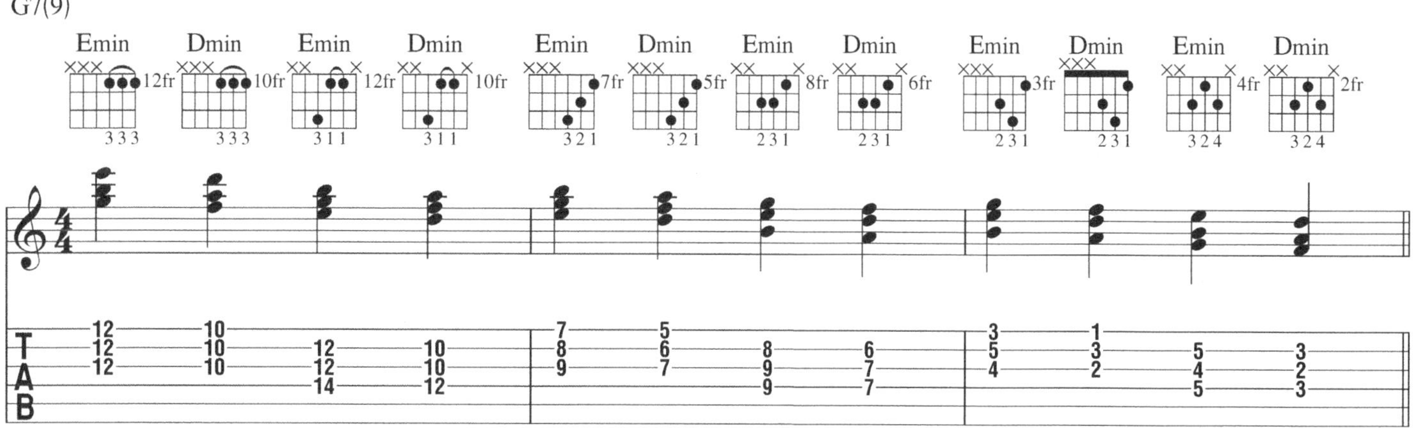

FIG. 10.2. Emin and Dmin in All Inversions Over G7

Note that the triads are all played on strings ④ ③ ② or ③ ② ①. Since the voicings include tensions, range is a consideration; too low would sound muddy and inappropriate. It's certainly possible to involve the lower string groups, but a rule of thumb is this: the lowest note that will sound as a tension is E on the second fret of the fourth string, seventh fret on the fifth string, or twelfth fret on the sixth string.

Playing through this etude will help you to put this set of triad pairs under your fingers.

13, 14

Gospel Blues

Rick Peckham

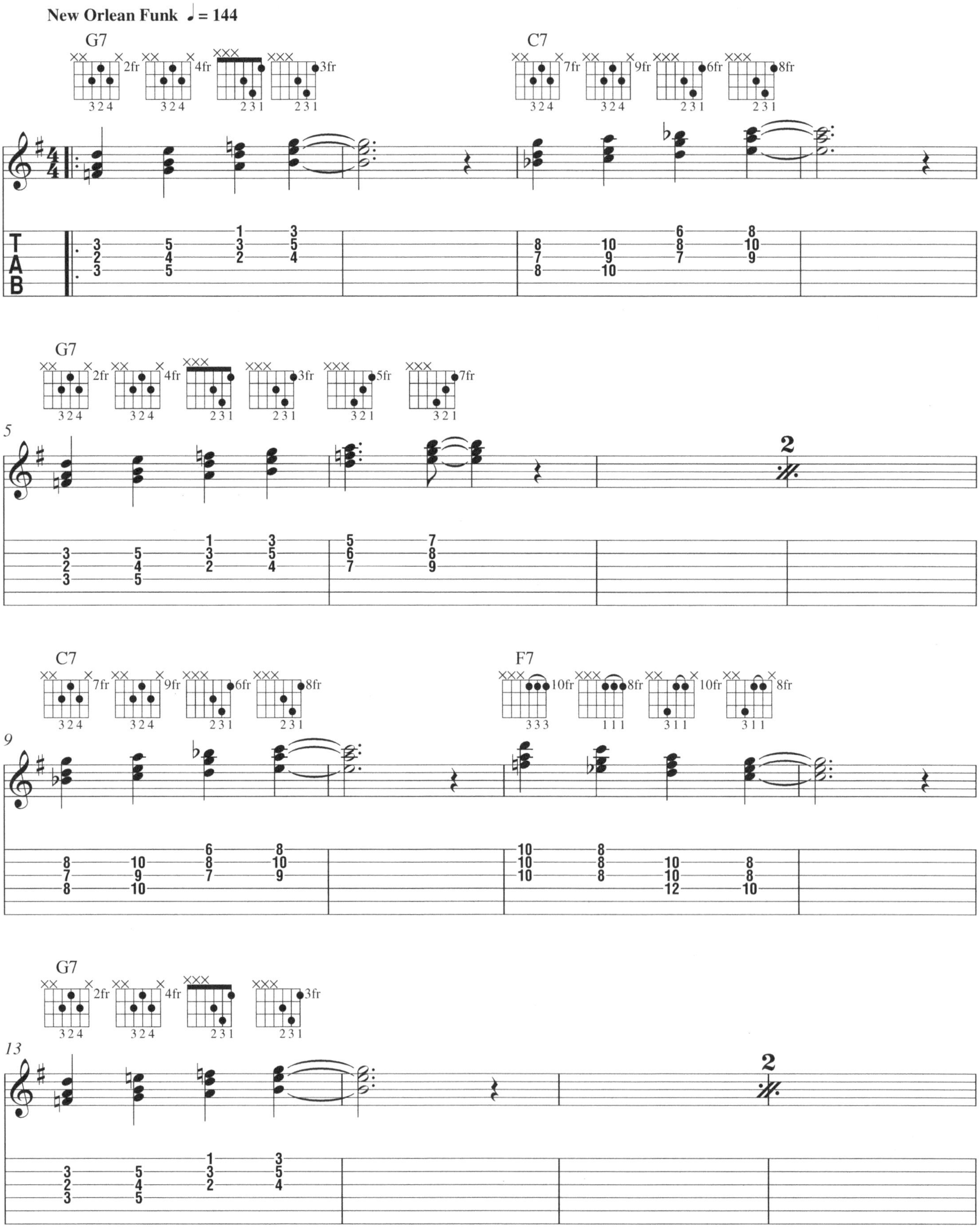

New Orlean Funk ♩ = 144

D7 C7

G7

D7 G13

FIG. 10.3. Gospel Blues Etude

GOSPEL SCALE

Some musicians describe the following as the "gospel scale," in the key of C.

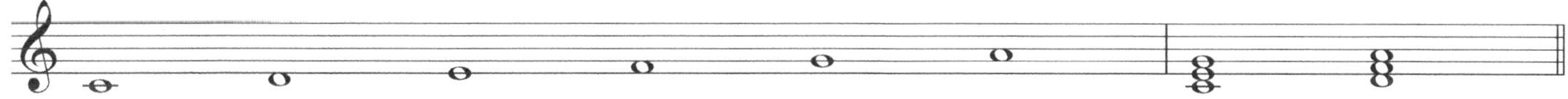

FIG. 10.4. Gospel Scale in C

This scale is a six-note or *hexatonic* scale that can be seen as a major pentatonic scale with an added 4 or as a diatonic major scale that's missing the leading tone (7). The scale consists of the notes of a C major and D minor triad.

The gospel scale has several other common names: the Grateful Dead scale, the bluegrass scale, and the Celtic scale. As you can see from the scale names, the major pentatonic scale with an added fourth has a lot of stylistic flexibility.

This triad pairing works well on extended periods of a single-chord vamp, for either one of its resident triads as the key center. Here is one possible way to pass through this scale harmonically, starting from open position up to the higher reaches of the fretboard.

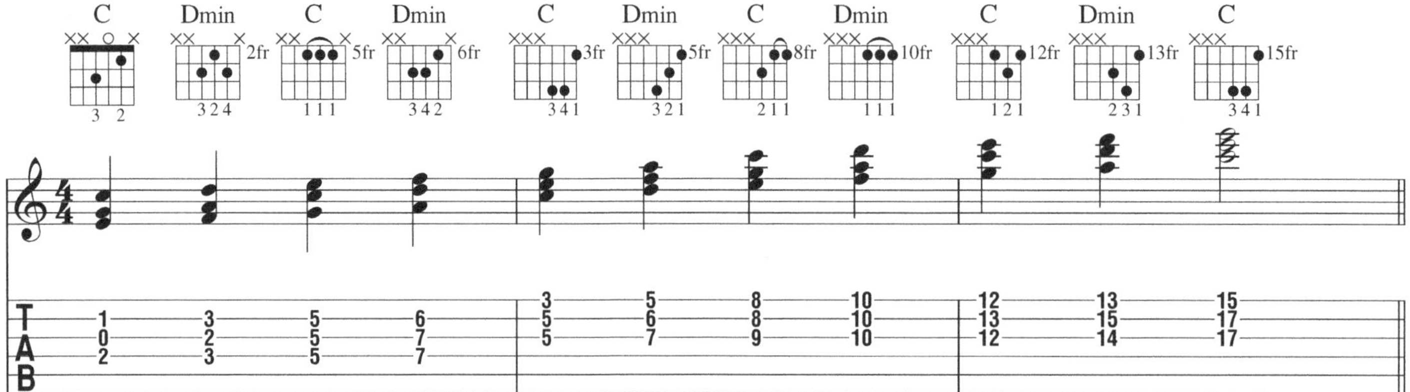

FIG. 10.5. Gospel Scale Progression

Play all inversions of C major and D minor, as above, alternating through the following pair of vamps. The major sound can be seen as Ionian (tonic major) or Mixolydian in color, whereas the vamp can be seen as Dorian (IImin function) or Aeolian (VImin function). Use all of the inversions, considering flow and use of interesting rhythms.

15, 16

FIG. 10.6. C Major and D Minor Vamp

Play through all of the inversions of the chords involved, and experiment with involving a D♯ (the ♯2 in C Ionian) as an approach to the third of the tonic major chord to achieve a bluesy effect. Guitarists often slide into chords chromatically, with the entire shape moving in parallel from a fret below. Pianists often restrict the chromatic approach to the third of the chord. It sounds unusual and attractive when played on the guitar in this way.

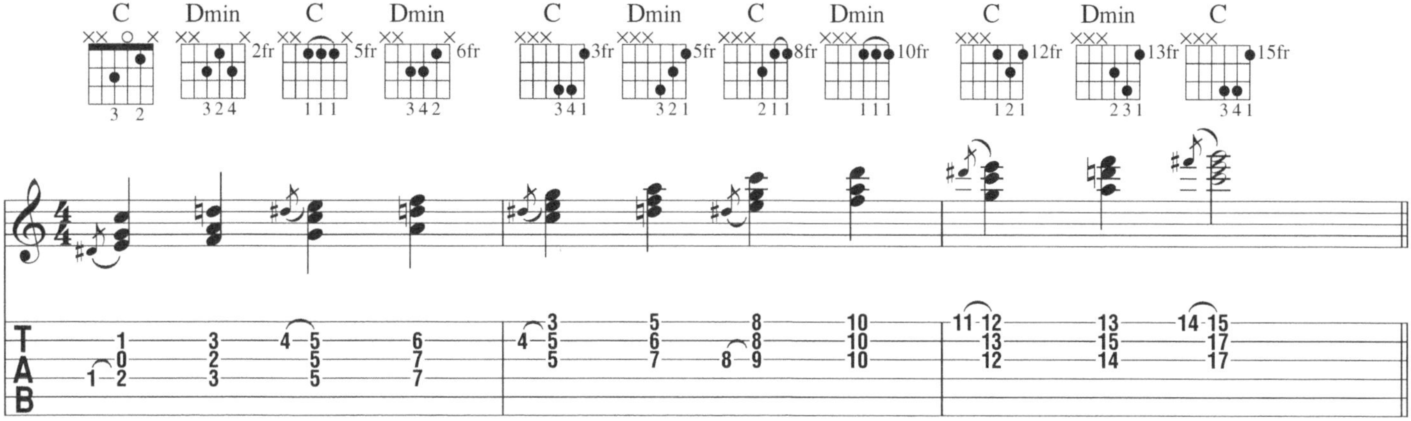

FIG. 10.7. C Major and D Minor Progression with ♯2 Approach to 3

CHAPTER 11

Quartal Voicings on min7♭5 Chords

The minor 7♭5 chord quality comes up frequently in jazz, rock, blues, and R&B styles. Contemporary jazz and post-bop styles often call for minor 7♭5 with a natural 9 as an available tension. An Fmin9♭5 is well served by use of A♭ melodic minor from F to F.

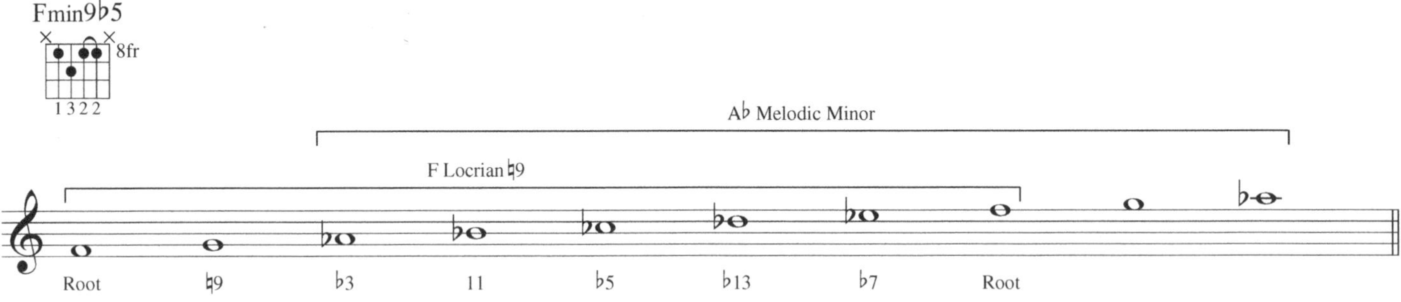

FIG. 11.1. A♭ Melodic Minor Over Fmin9♭5

B♭ minor 6 pentatonic contains the essence of the sound of Fmin9♭5, and it is contained by this scale.

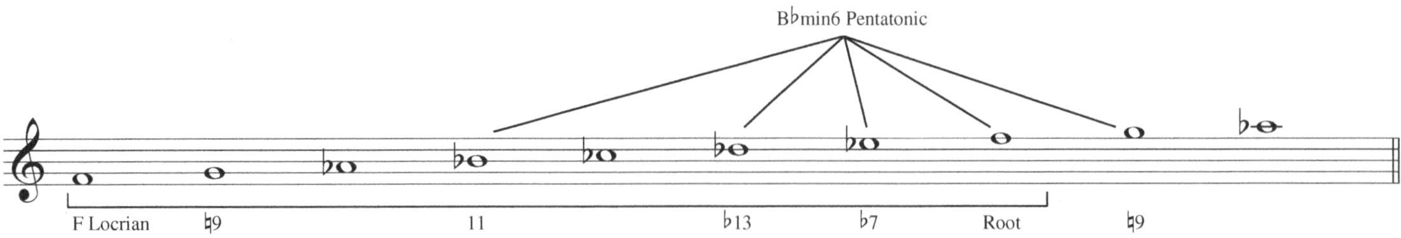

FIG. 11.2. B♭min6 Pentatonic Over Fmin9♭5

Let's use B♭ minor 6 pentatonic as a lead line, harmonized by the seven notes of A♭ melodic minor/F Locrian natural 9.

FIG. 11.3. B♭min6 Pentatonic Lead Line

Here are the voicings that work well on Fmin9♭5, using B♭ minor 6 pentatonic as a lead line, harmonized with the notes of A♭ melodic minor. Note the "So What" shape found in the first two voicings, harmonizing the root and second degree. Enharmonic descriptions of the voicings appear under each chord.

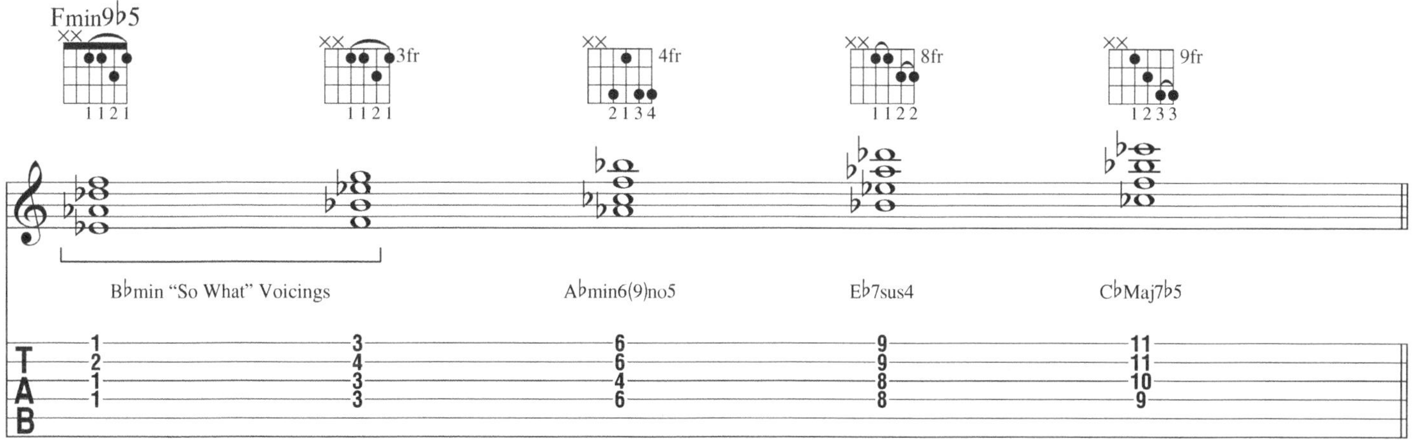

FIG. 11.4. Minor 6 Pentatonic Lead Line with Melodic Minor Harmony on Top Four Lines

Play through min7♭5 chords using these new modal sounds, through twelve keys. You need to teach yourself the way that the various shapes feel under your fingers to gain control of these interesting sounds. In the backing track provided, play the notated voicings in order, and then improvise, working to gain fluency with this set of suggested shapes. The guitar demo track (track 17) goes up and down each notated shape on the top set of four strings. Play along this way, then vary at will with the track containing accompaniment only (track 18).

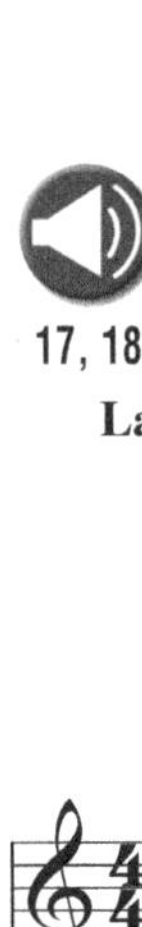

17, 18

Latin ♩ = 176

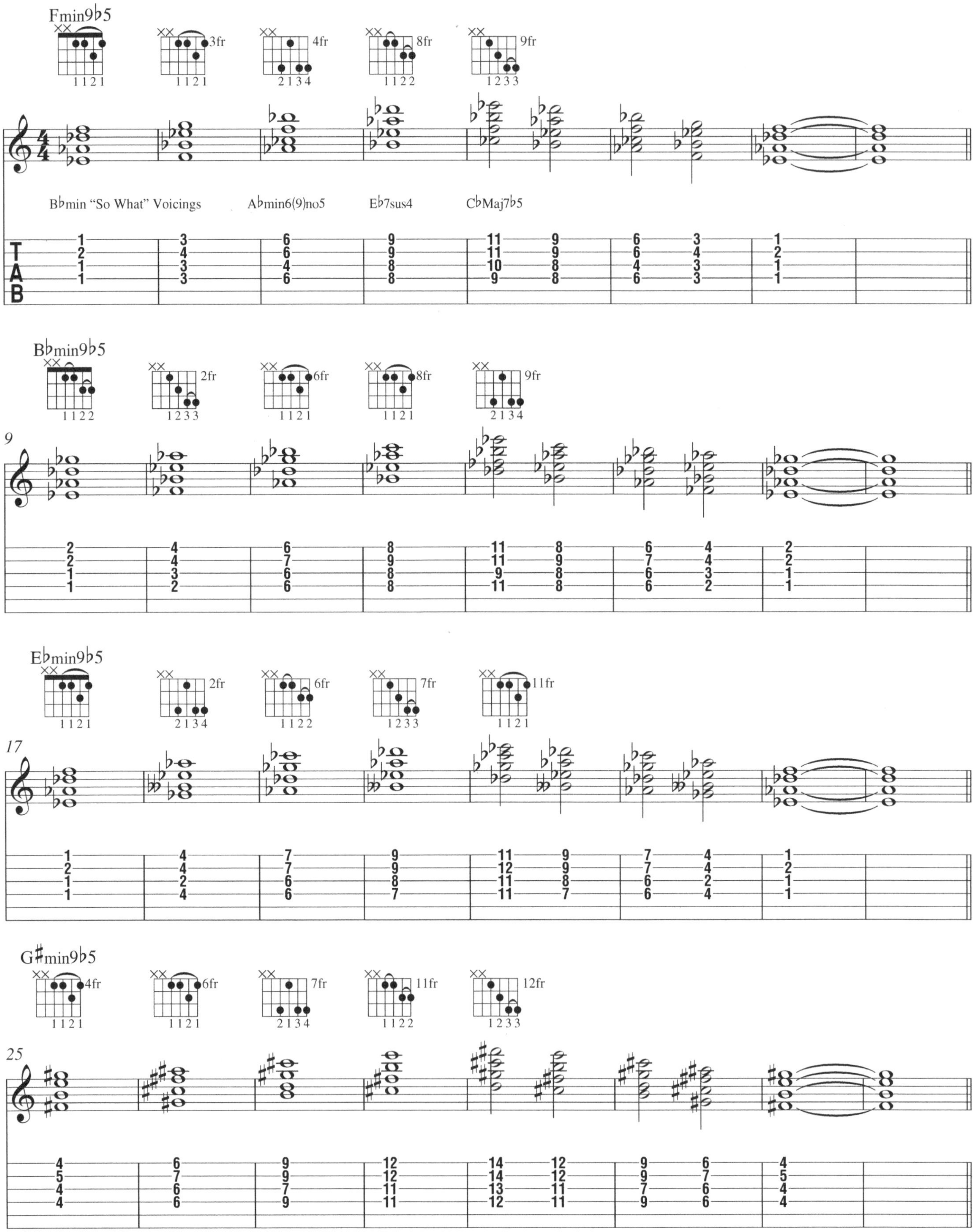

Fmin9♭5

B♭min "So What" Voicings A♭min6(9)no5 E♭7sus4 C♭Maj7♭5

B♭min9♭5

9

E♭min9♭5

17

G♯min9♭5

25

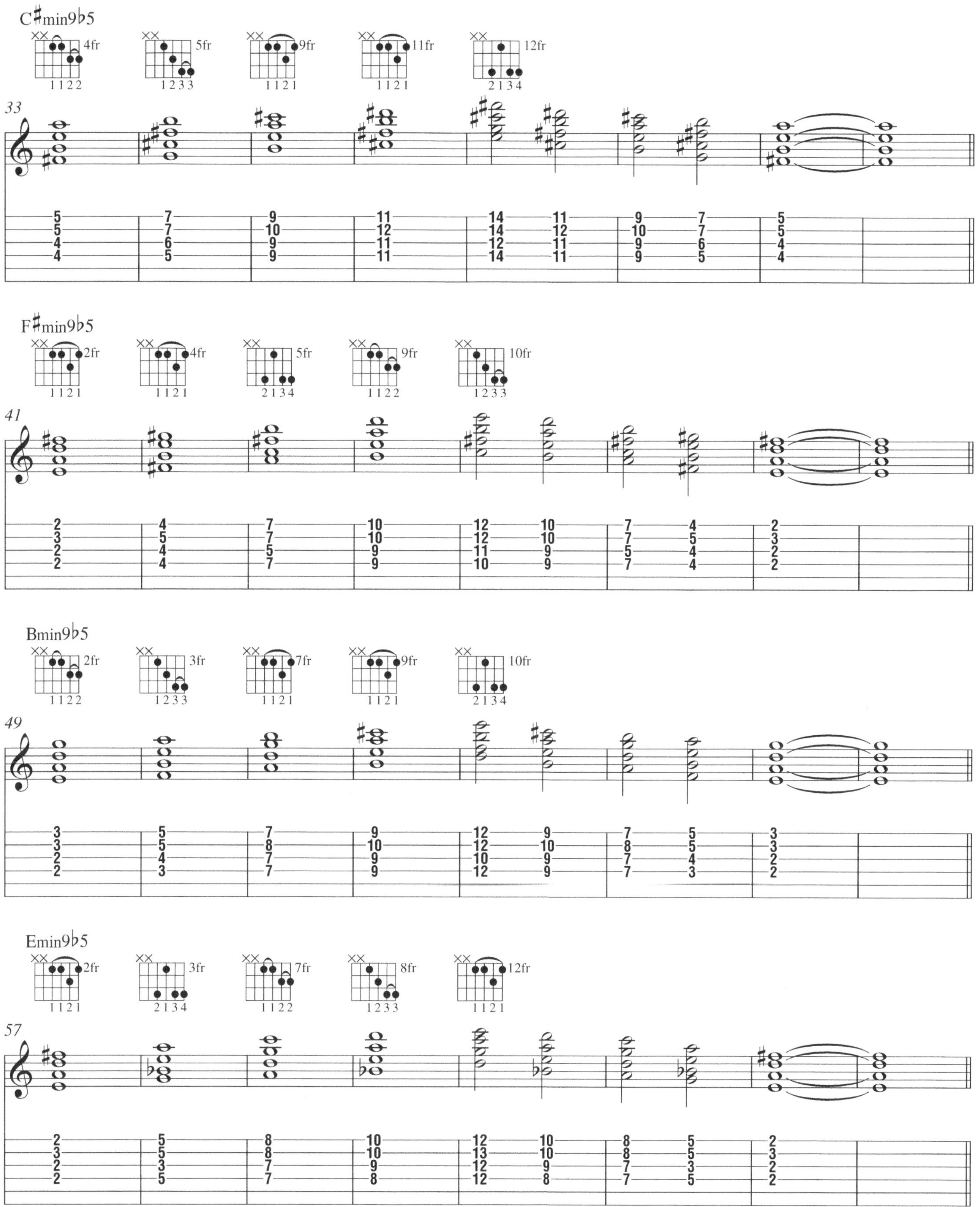
C♯min9♭5
4fr
5fr
9fr
11fr
12fr
F♯min9♭5
2fr
4fr
5fr
9fr
10fr
Bmin9♭5
2fr
3fr
7fr
9fr
10fr
Emin9♭5
2fr
3fr
7fr
8fr
12fr

FIG. 11.5. Min7♭5 Using Quartal Sounds in Twelve Keys

The previous etude emphasizes the melodic minor harmony and minor 6 pentatonic lead line on strings ④ ③ ② ①. It is possible to play the voicings on other string sets too. Here are more options for you to use on the previous etude.

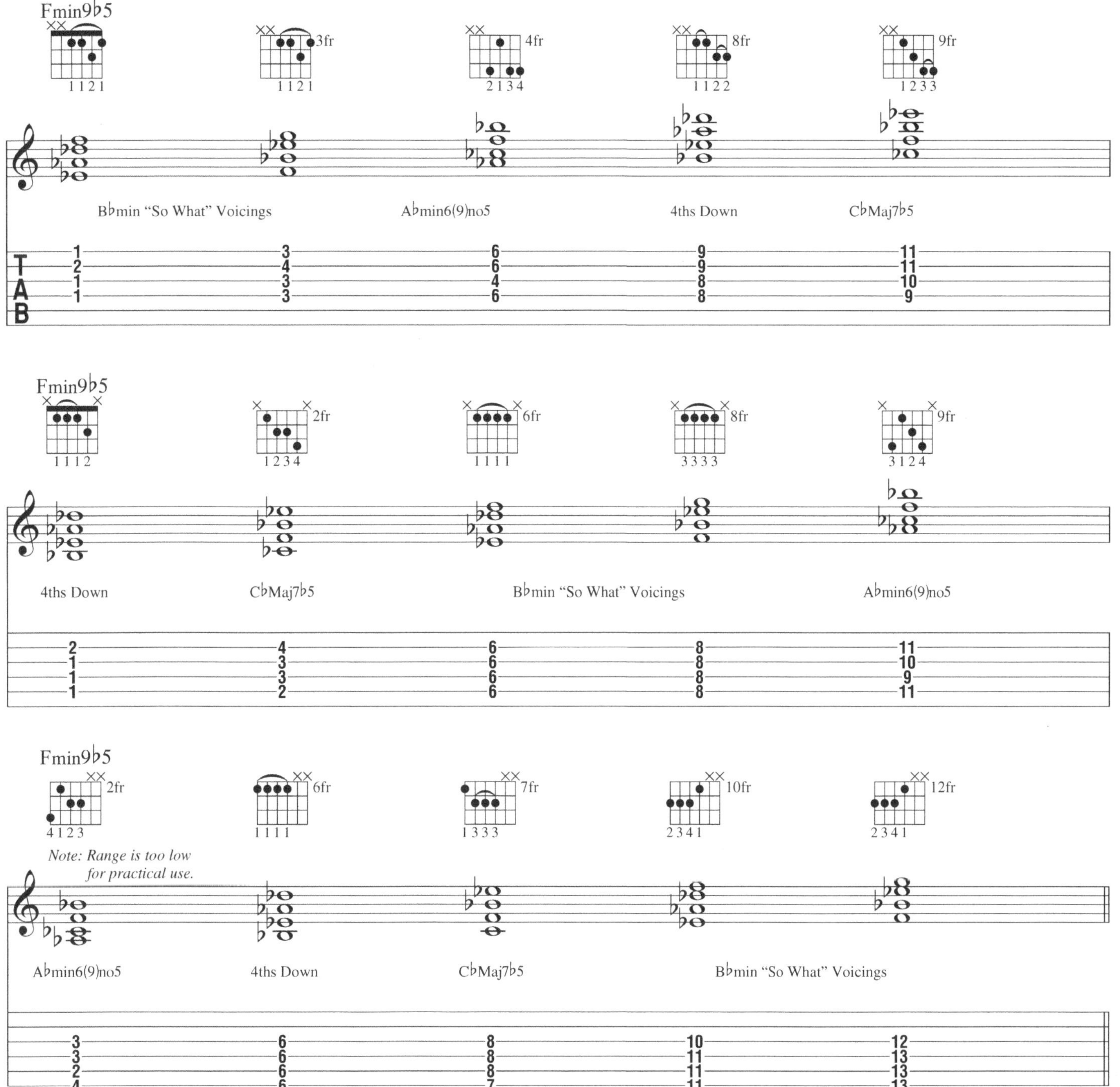

FIG. 11.6. Minor 6 Pentatonic Lead Line Melodic Minor Harmony on All String Sets

For the voicings to sound properly, it's best to ensure that the tensions are played above middle C. If the range of a voicing is too low, it can sound muddy and undesirable. That's why the upper string sets are emphasized throughout this book. You may also wish to establish the chord sound with a traditional drop-2 or drop-3 voicing for the chord in question before exploring the sound modally.

CHAPTER 12

Modal Voicings on Major Chords

Here are the notes of a C major pentatonic scale, analyzed with respect to a C major chord.

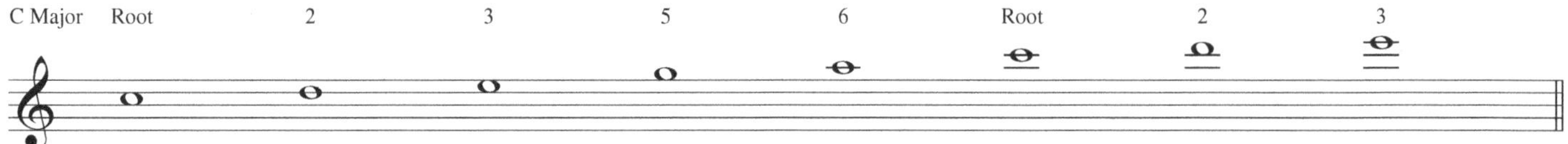

FIG. 12.1. C Major Pentatonic Scale

Let's use C major pentatonic as a lead line, harmonized with the seven-note diatonic scale, with the 5 of the chord on the third fret of the first string. This set of shapes will work well on a major sound.

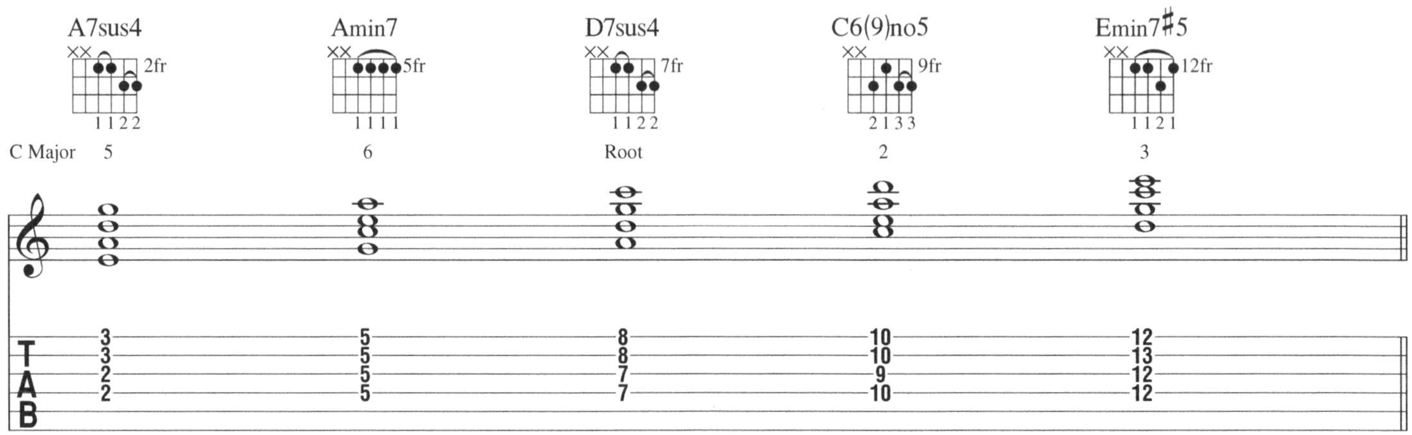

FIG. 12.2. C Major Pentatonic Lead Line Harmonized with Seven-Note Diatonic Scale

G major pentatonic is another common scale choice that works well over a C major chord.

FIG. 12.3. G Major Pentatonic over C Major

Here's a good way to use the seven-note diatonic major scale with this five-note lead line. These voicings work well for an extended period of C major.

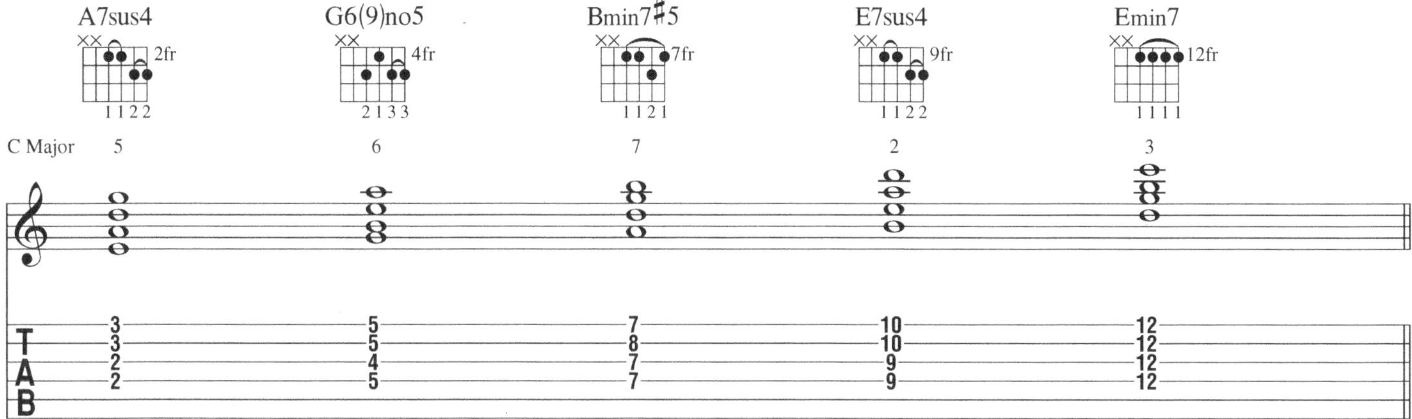

FIG. 12.4. G Major Pentatonic Lead Line Harmonized with Seven-Note Diatonic Scale

Finally, superimposing D major pentatonic on a C major chord brings out the ♯11 sound.

Here are the notes of a D major pentatonic, including the notes that we'll be using on the first string.

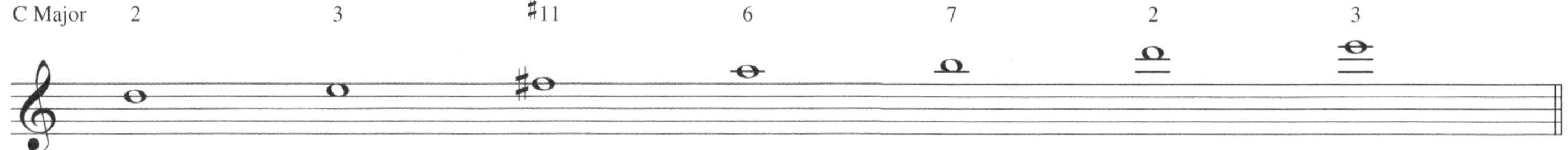

FIG. 12.5. D Major Pentatonic Scale over C Major

Here are the pentatonic lead line voicings, transposing the material to D major.

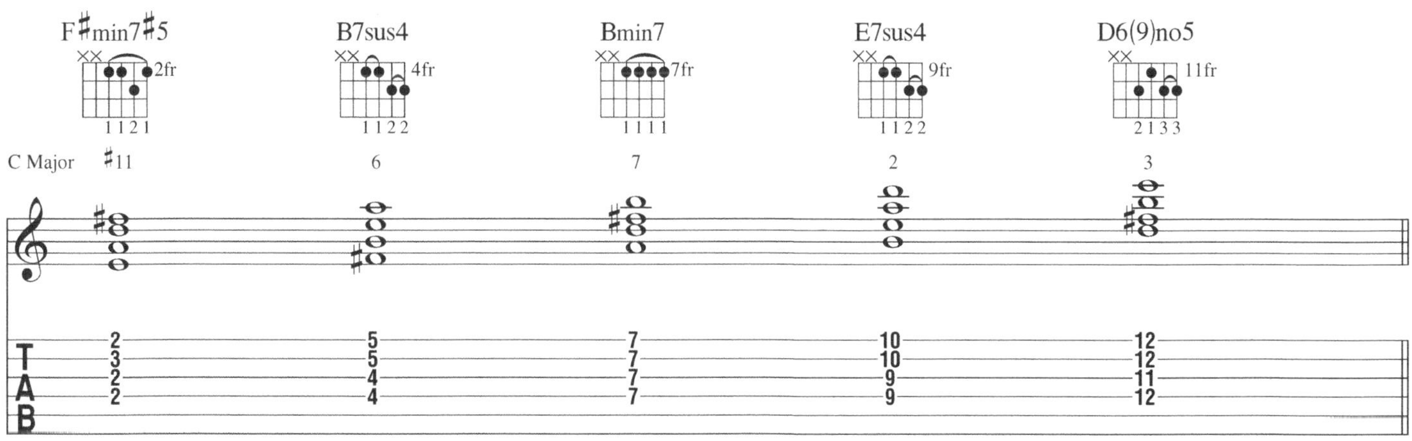

FIG. 12.6. D Major Pentatonic Lead Line Voicings

Play through all twelve keys with the track provided. Experiment with pentatonic from the tonic, pentatonic from the fifth and pentatonic from the second in each key. In the audio demonstration, I demonstrate the major pentatonic from the fifth degree and the major pentatonic from the second degree in each of the keys.

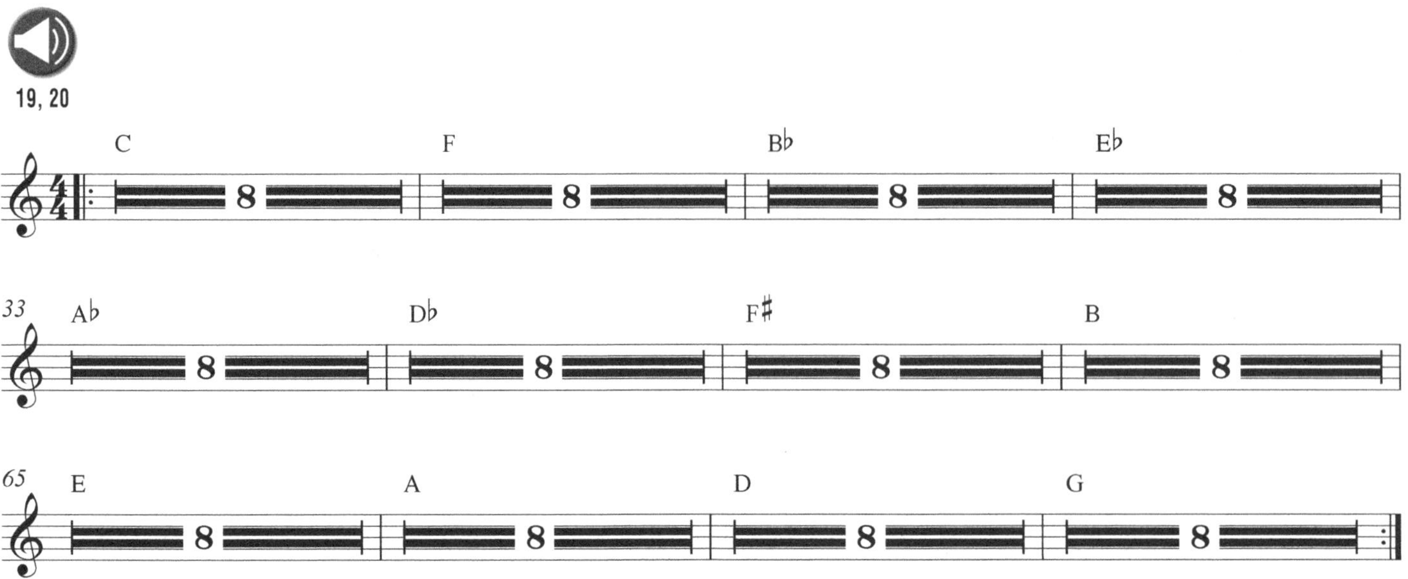

FIG. 12.7. Major Pentatonic Groove through Twelve Keys

CHAPTER 13

Maj7♭5 Used in Several Ways

The quartal voicing found on the fourth degree of the major scale consists of an augmented fourth followed by two perfect fourths. Typically seen as Maj7♭5, this configuration of notes can be also be found in melodic minor.

In figure 13.1, the A♭Maj7♭5 chord is shown in both drop-2 and close-position shapes, as found on the fourth mode of E♭ major.

FIG. 13.1. A♭Maj7♭5: Drop 2 Voicing and Close Voicing

Here is the same chord, as built on the flatted-third degree of F melodic minor.

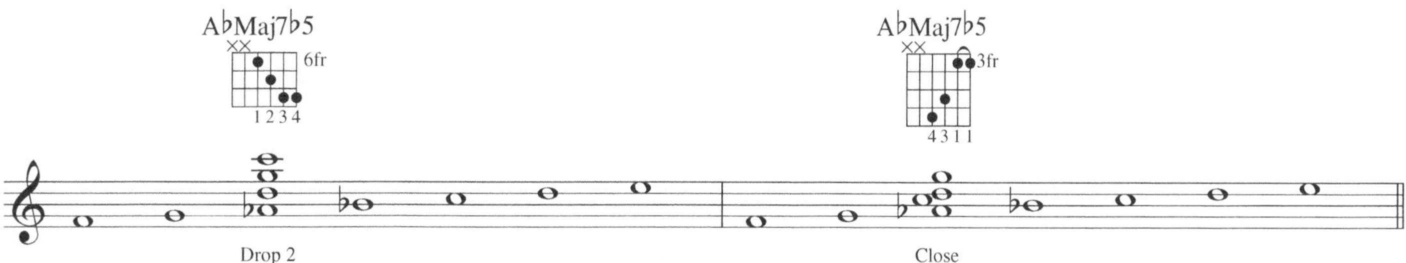

FIG. 13.2. Quartal Voicing on the ♭3 of F Melodic Minor

The ability to play only a few notes while implying a tall harmonic structure is appealing to many guitarists. There are at least six ways to use this particular set of notes, many bringing out interesting tensions, while requiring little physical effort.

Placing the chord on different degrees will result in the following sounds. The first two result from diatonic major. The remaining four are implied by melodic minor chordal sounds.

SIX IDENTITIES FOR A♭MAJ7♭5

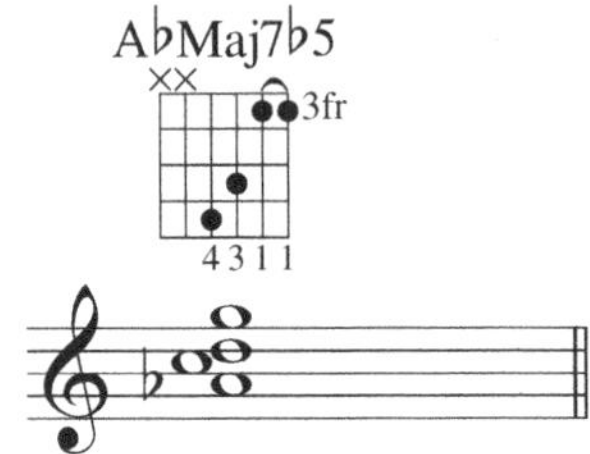

FIG. 13.3. A♭Maj7♭5

Moving A♭Maj7♭5 to the degrees listed can imply the following sounds:

DEGREE	IMPLIED SOUND
I	A♭Maj7♭5
♭VII	B♭7(9,13)
♭III	Fmin6(9)
III	E7(♯9, ♯5)
♭V	Dmin11♭5
♭II	Gsus(♭9)

Since the listener is intended to hear these notes as tensions, it's important to play them in the mid to upper range of the guitar.

Moving this structure around, here are the six sounds again, this time using C as the root of the implied sound.

For This Implied Sound...	Use This...	
	Chord	Degree
CMaj7♭5	CMaj7♭5	I
C7(9,13)	B♭Maj7♭5	♭VII
Cmin6(9)	E♭Maj7♭5	♭III
C7(♯9, ♯5)	EMaj7♭5	III
Cmin7♭5	G♭Maj7♭5	♭V
Csus4(♭9)	D♭Maj7♭5	♭II

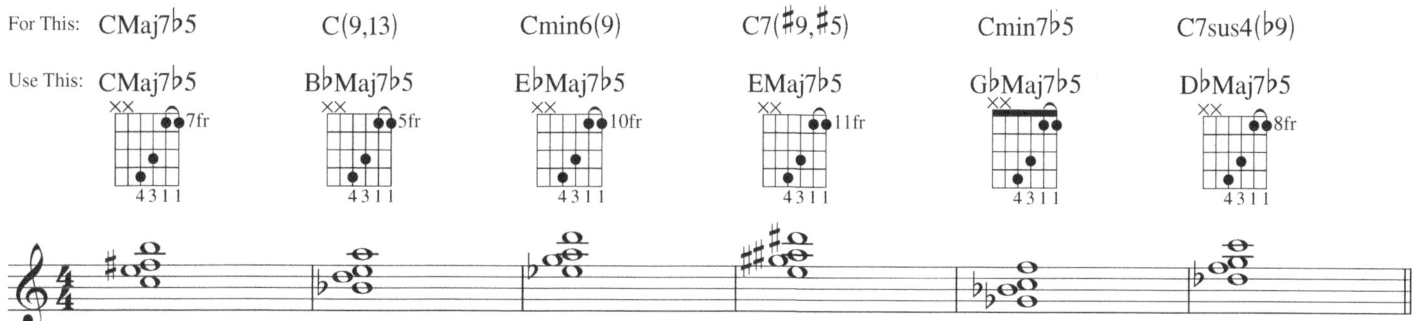

FIG. 13.4. Moving Maj7♭5 Voicing to Imply Various Harmonic Sounds

Close-position works well with Maj7♭5 voicings, as this particular shape is easily played on the top four strings of the guitar. All inversions (as well as drop 2) are worth exploring, but since tensions are often involved, it's often best to keep them on the top four or (at the lowest) middle four string sets. Try them as demonstrated here with three choruses of B♭ blues. The original, most basic, chord symbol is found in the staff, while the voicing implying desirable tensions is found above.

B♭ Blues Practice

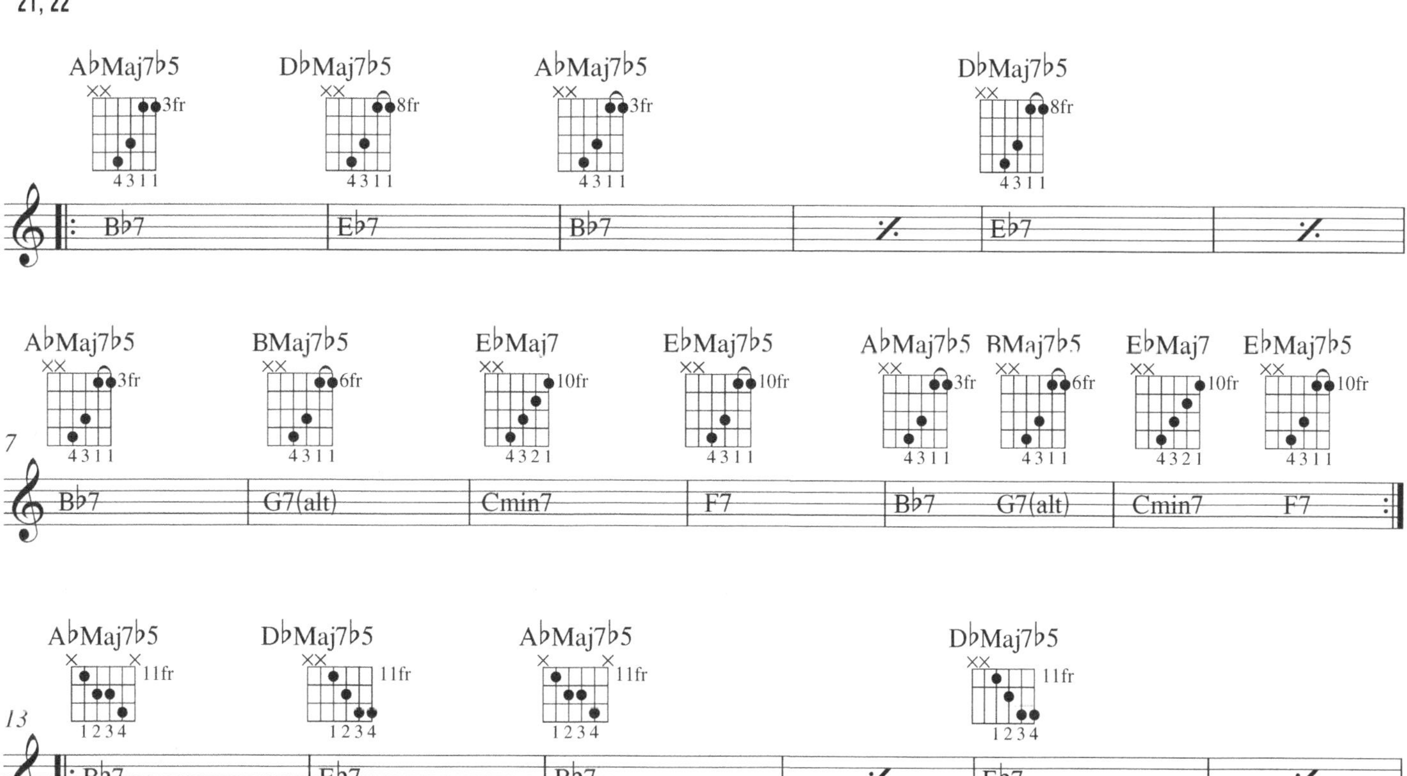

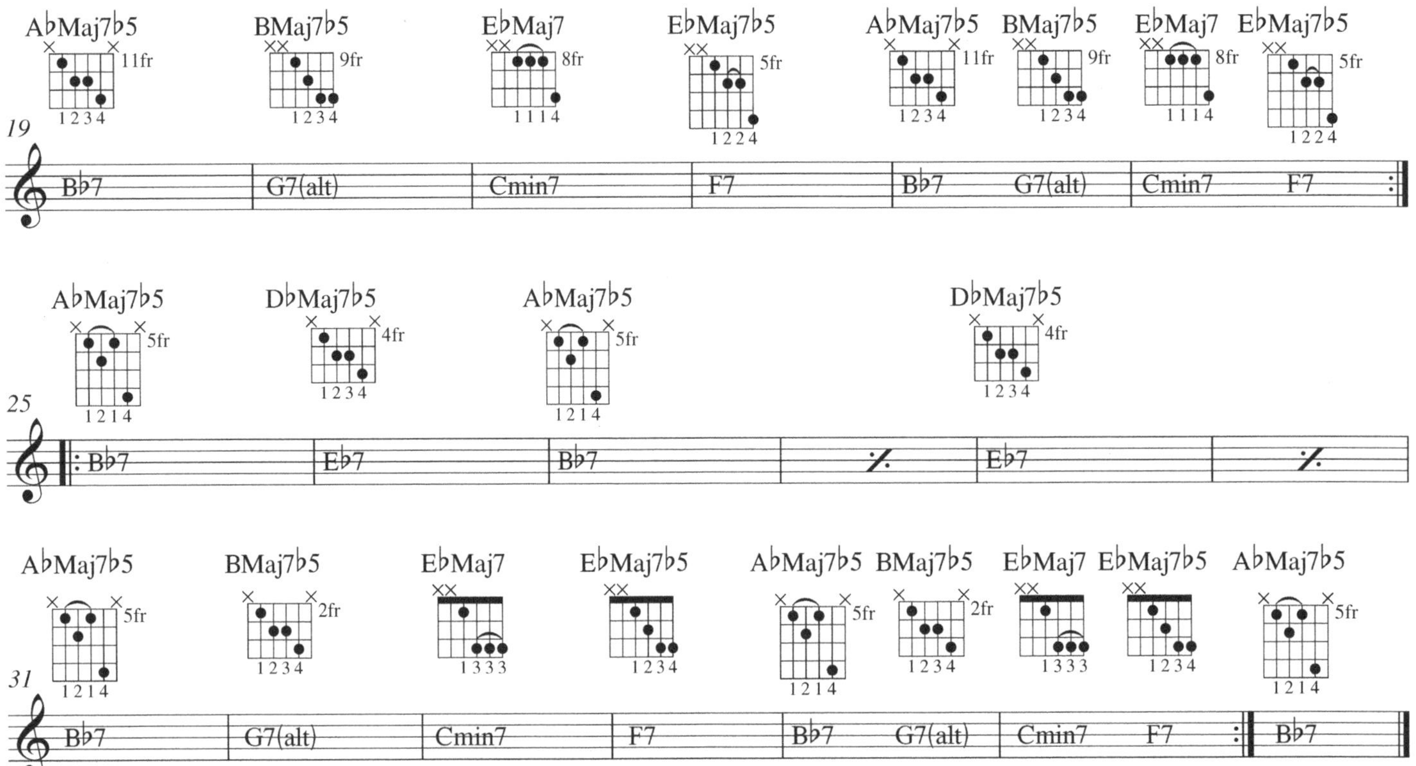

FIG. 13.5. B♭ Blues Using Maj7♭5 Structures

NOTE: The Maj7♭5 shape is also found on the ♭6 of harmonic minor, and you may wish to explore the implications of that set of sounds as well.

CHAPTER 14

Melodic Minor, Harmonic Minor, Harmonic Major, and Diminished for Quartal Sounds

Beyond the diatonic major scale and its modes, Berklee's guitar students are required to learn the following scales:

- melodic minor
- harmonic minor
- harmonic major
- diminished
- whole tone

It is possible to find quartal sounds in all of the above, except for the whole tone scale, so let's look at all of the rest of the scales listed.

Using a fretboard diagram approach, here's a review of quartal shapes from C major, from the perspective of D Dorian. Let's follow the shapes of C major, traveling up the fretboard on various string groups in standard tuning on the guitar. The scale is started in diatonic fourths on each string group from the lowest voicing possible, not including open strings.

The voicings here work best for sustained periods of Dmin7 or G7sus4, but also work for the related chords of C Major: CMaj7, Dmin7(9,11,13), Emin7(♭9,11,♭13), FMaj7(9,♯11,13), G7(9,13), Amin7(9,11,♭13), Bmin7♭5.

C Major (D Dorian) in Fourths ⑤ ④ ③ ②

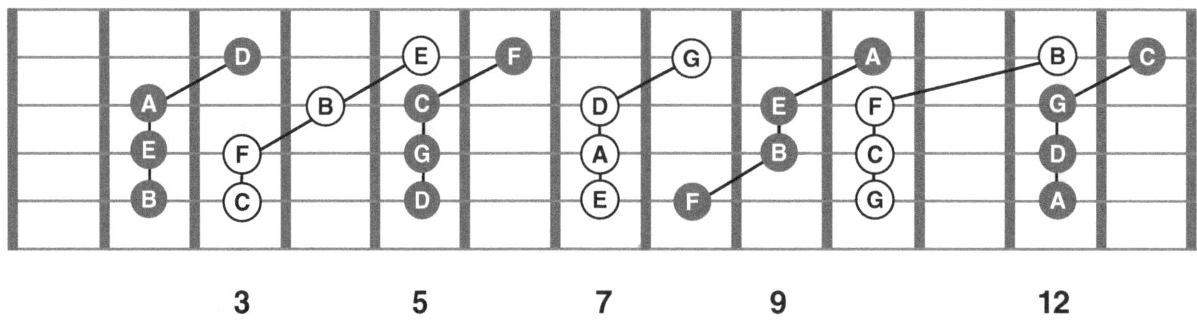

C Major (D Dorian) in Fourths ④ ③ ② ①

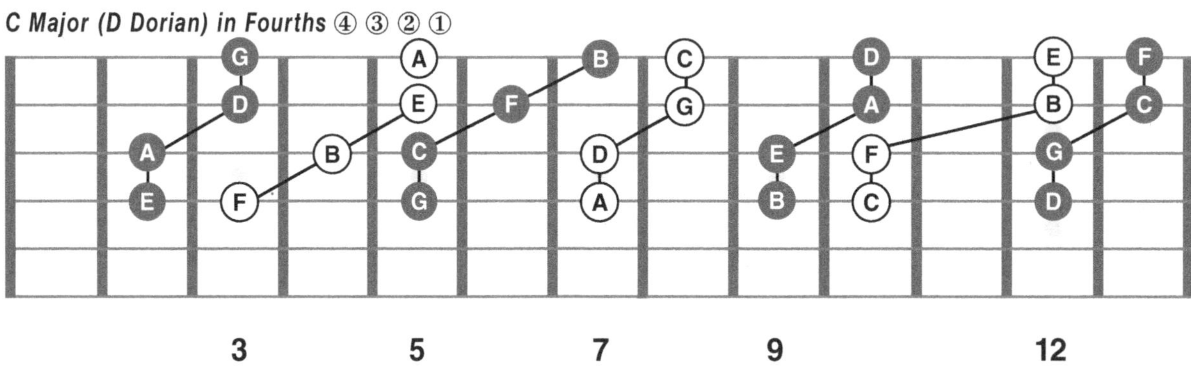

C Major (D Dorian) in Fourths ⑥ ⑤ ④ ③

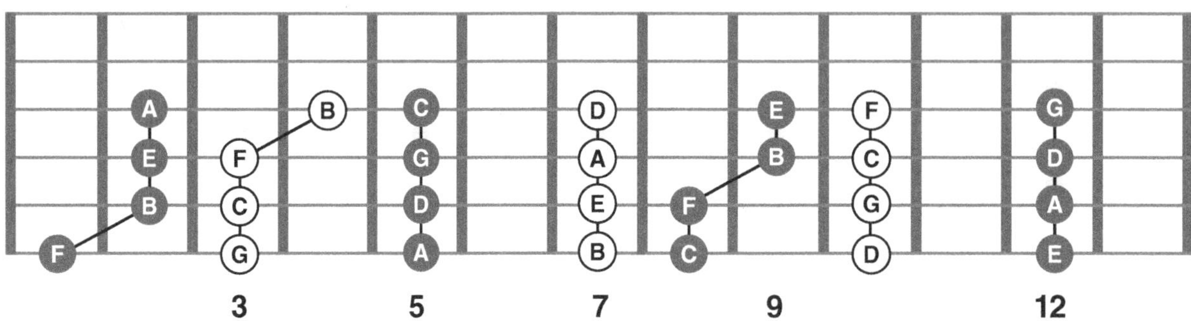

FIG. 14.1. D Dorian in Fourths

The lowest set of four strings may sound too muddy and dark for many musical purposes, but there are some beautiful colors to be found there.

MELODIC MINOR

C melodic minor can also produce some very useful sounds using modal/quartal shapes. The lowest voicing on the middle set of four strings yields a dominant 7 voicing with ♯9, frequently called the "Hendrix chord."

These voicings can work for sustained passages using the following chord qualities: Cmin(Maj7), Dsus(♭9), E♭Maj7(♯5), F7(9,♯11,13), G7(9,♭13), Amin7♭5(9), B7(alt).

C Melodic Minor in Fourths ⑤ ④ ③ ②

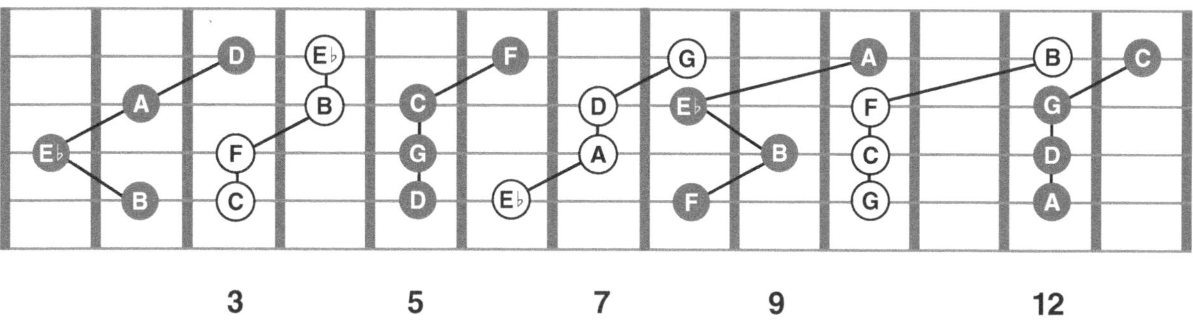

C Melodic Minor in Fourths ④ ③ ② ①

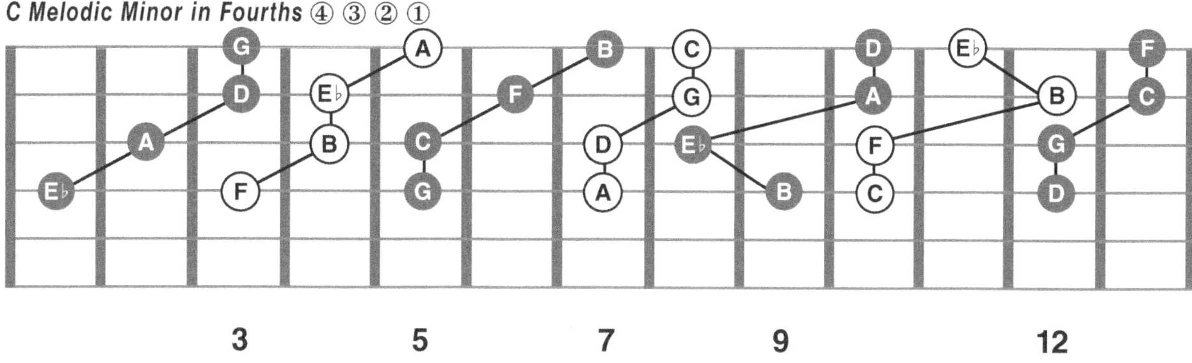

C Melodic Minor in Fourths ⑥ ⑤ ④ ③

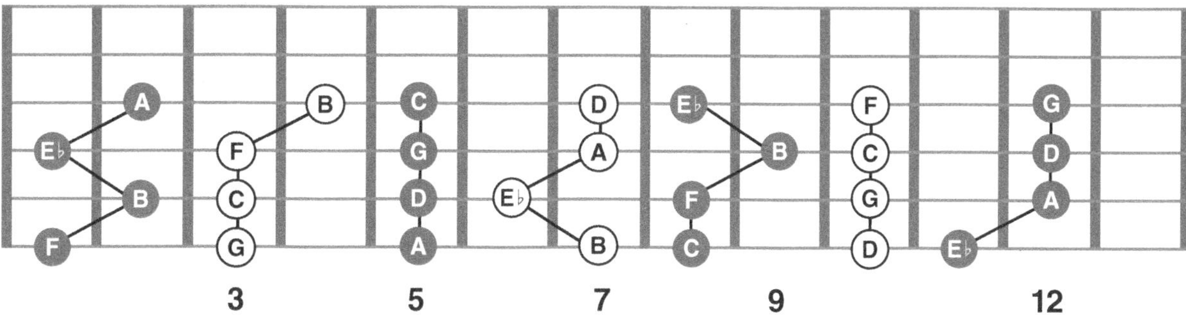

FIG. 14.2. C Melodic Minor in Fourths

HARMONIC MINOR

The harmonic minor scale is particularly helpful with extended periods of dominant 7(♭9,♭13). Making the adjustment from the melodic minor quartal shapes to harmonic minor is merely a matter of moving the natural 6 to flat 6. Note the diatonic appearance of A♭Maj7♭5 in a drop-2 shape.

C Harmonic Minor in Fourths ⑤ ④ ③ ②

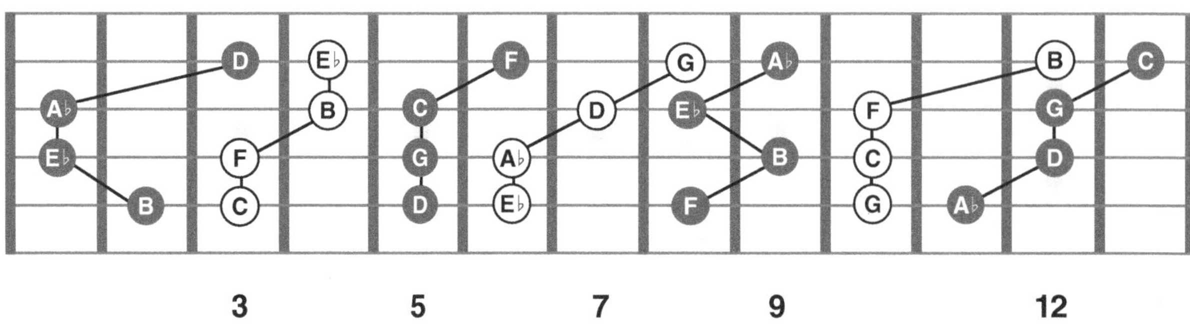

C Harmonic Minor in Fourths ④ ③ ② ①

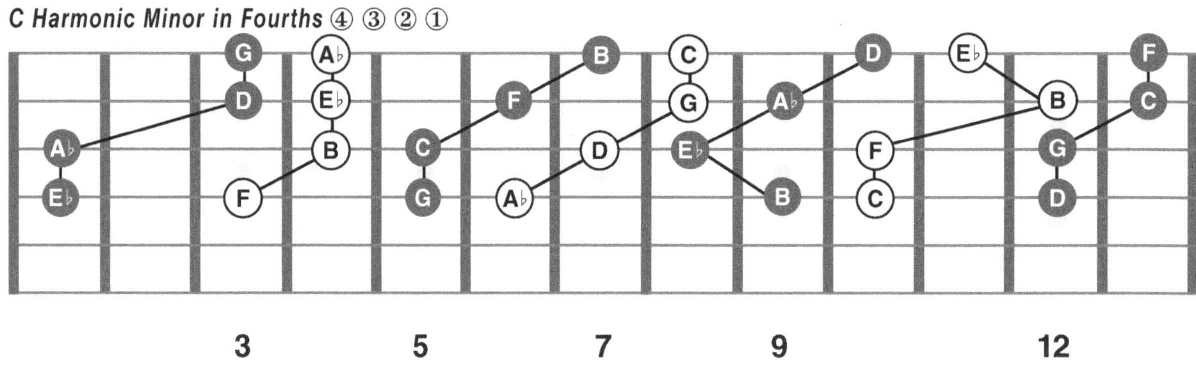

C Harmonic Minor in Fourths ⑥ ⑤ ④ ③

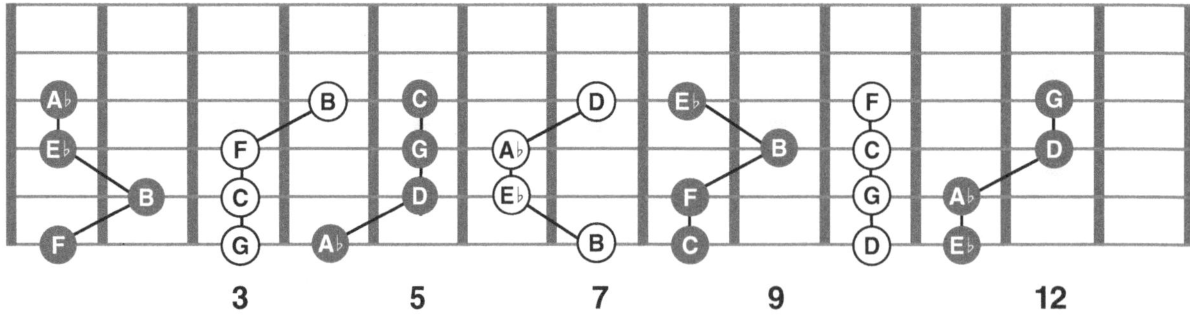

FIG. 14.3. C Harmonic Minor in Fourths

HARMONIC MAJOR

Guitar Department Professor Mick Goodrick introduced the harmonic major scale into the Berklee Guitar Department's scale vocabulary in the 1990s. Mick's influence has loomed large at Berklee, in Boston, and in the guitar world in general. Compared to the diatonic major scale, melodic minor contains the ♭3, and harmonic minor contains ♭3 and ♭6. Harmonic major can be seen as a mirror opposite of melodic minor, only one note away from diatonic major. It can be seen as major with a ♭6.

	Major Scale (natural 3, natural 6)	
Melodic Minor (same notes as major with a ♭3)		**Harmonic Major (same notes as major with a ♭6)**
	Harmonic Minor (same notes as major with a ♭3 and ♭6)	

To construct quartal sounds using harmonic major, make adjustments to include the major 3 and ♭6 degrees. It's one note removed from diatonic major, melodic minor, or harmonic minor, but yields some different colors. It is perhaps most useful from its third and fourth degrees, E7(♯9) and Fdim(Maj7). Here are the diatonic quartal voicings from C harmonic major.

Chords implied here: CMaj7(9,♭13), Dmin7♭5, E7(♭9,♯9), Fdim(Maj7), G7(♭9,13), A♭dim(Maj7), Bdim7.

C Harmonic Major in Fourths ⑤ ④ ③ ②

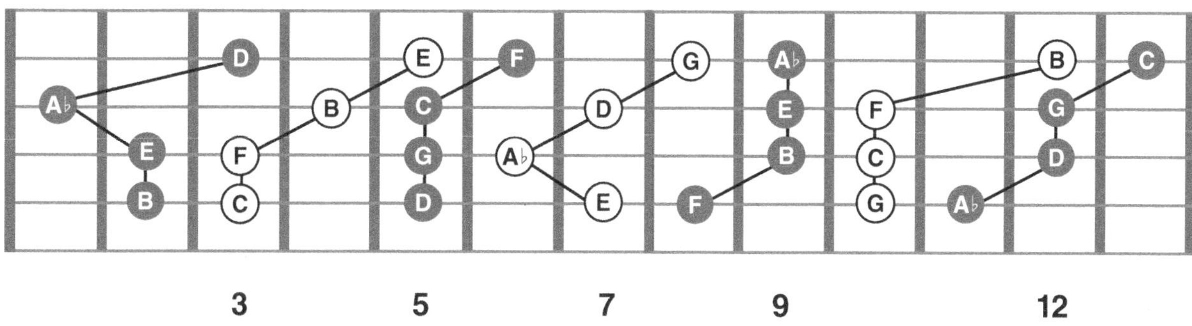

C Harmonic Major in Fourths ④ ③ ② ①

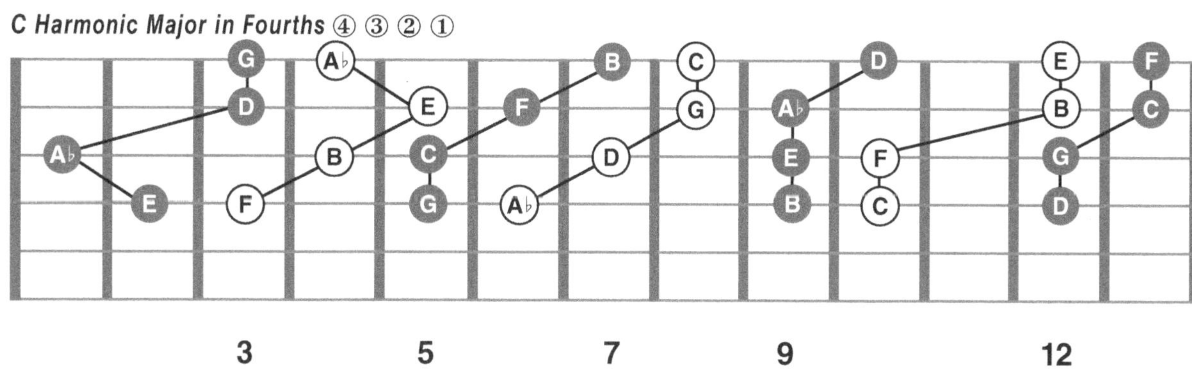

C Harmonic Major in Fourths ⑥ ⑤ ④ ③

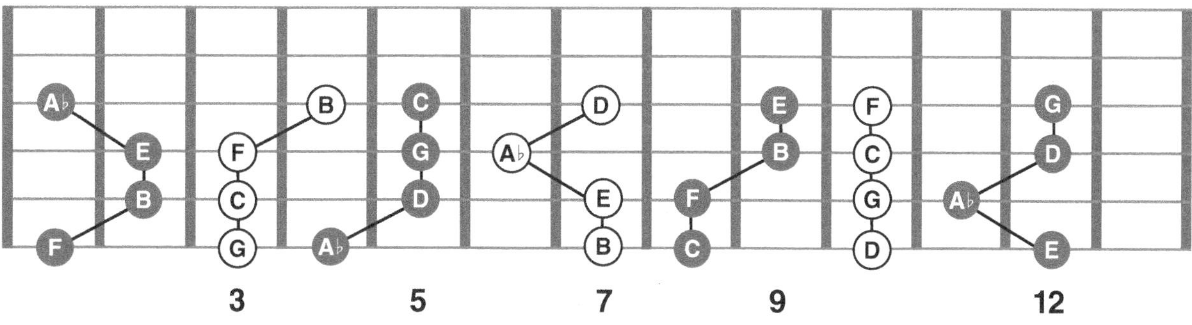

FIG. 14.4. C Harmonic Major in Fourths

DIMINISHED SCALE

Finding quartal sounds within the diminished scale (whole step/half step) or its other mode, the symmetrical diminished (half step/whole step), is a little challenging, but it isn't impossible. Starting with Cdim(Maj7) and keeping one note in common allows us to symmetrically climb up the scale, alternating dim(Maj7) with dominant 7(♯9) voicings. Use of this set of voicings can work over extended periods of diminished 7 colors. The voicings here work for Cdim7, E♭dim7, G♭dim7, and Adim7.

Modal Sounds from C W/H Diminished Scale

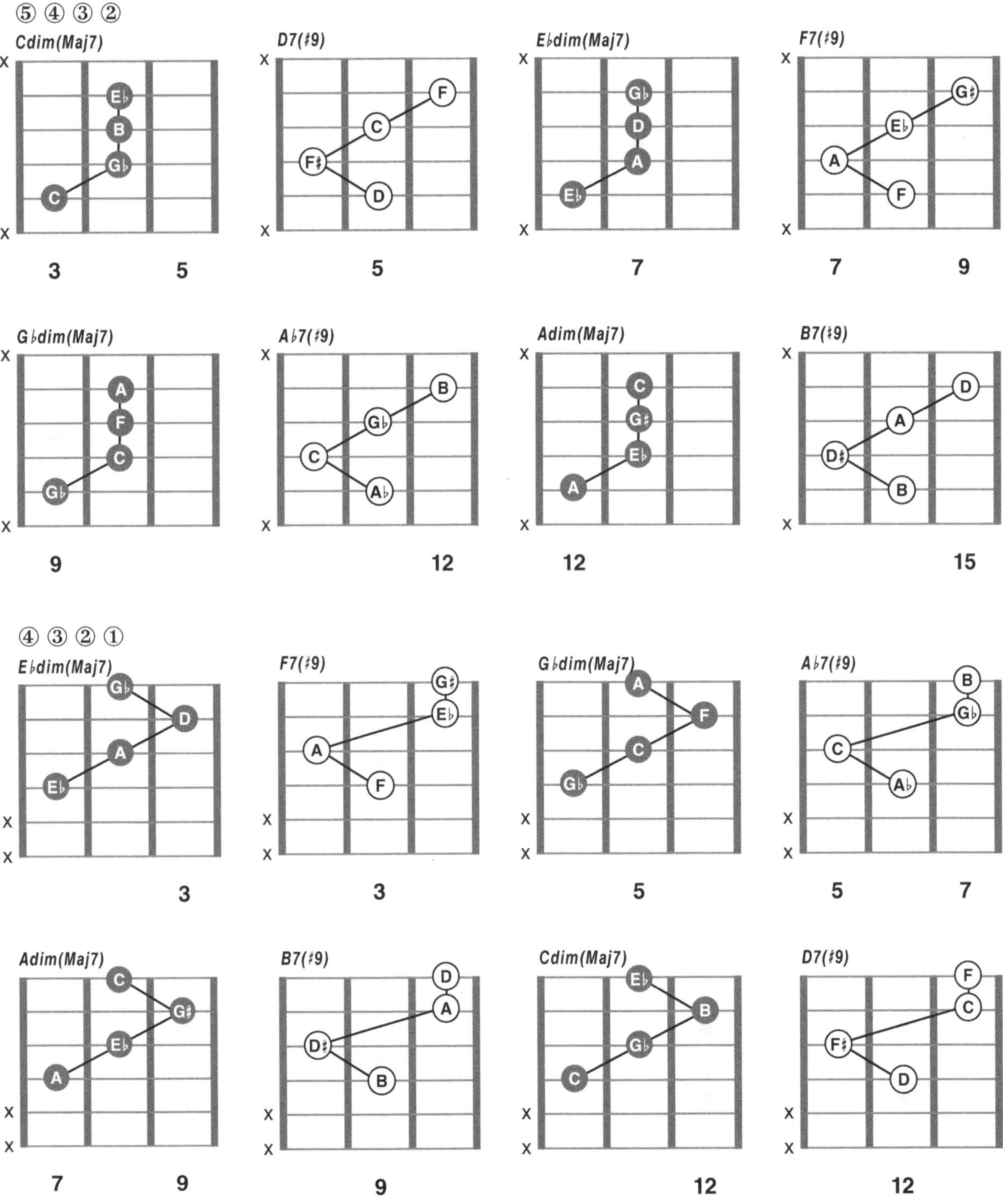

FIG. 14.5. C Whole/Half Diminished in Fourths

On the other side of the coin, it's possible to interpret the scale similarly, using the 7(♯9) as "home," alternating with dim(Maj7). These shapes will work with C7(♯9), E♭7(♯9), F♯7(♯9), A7(♯9).

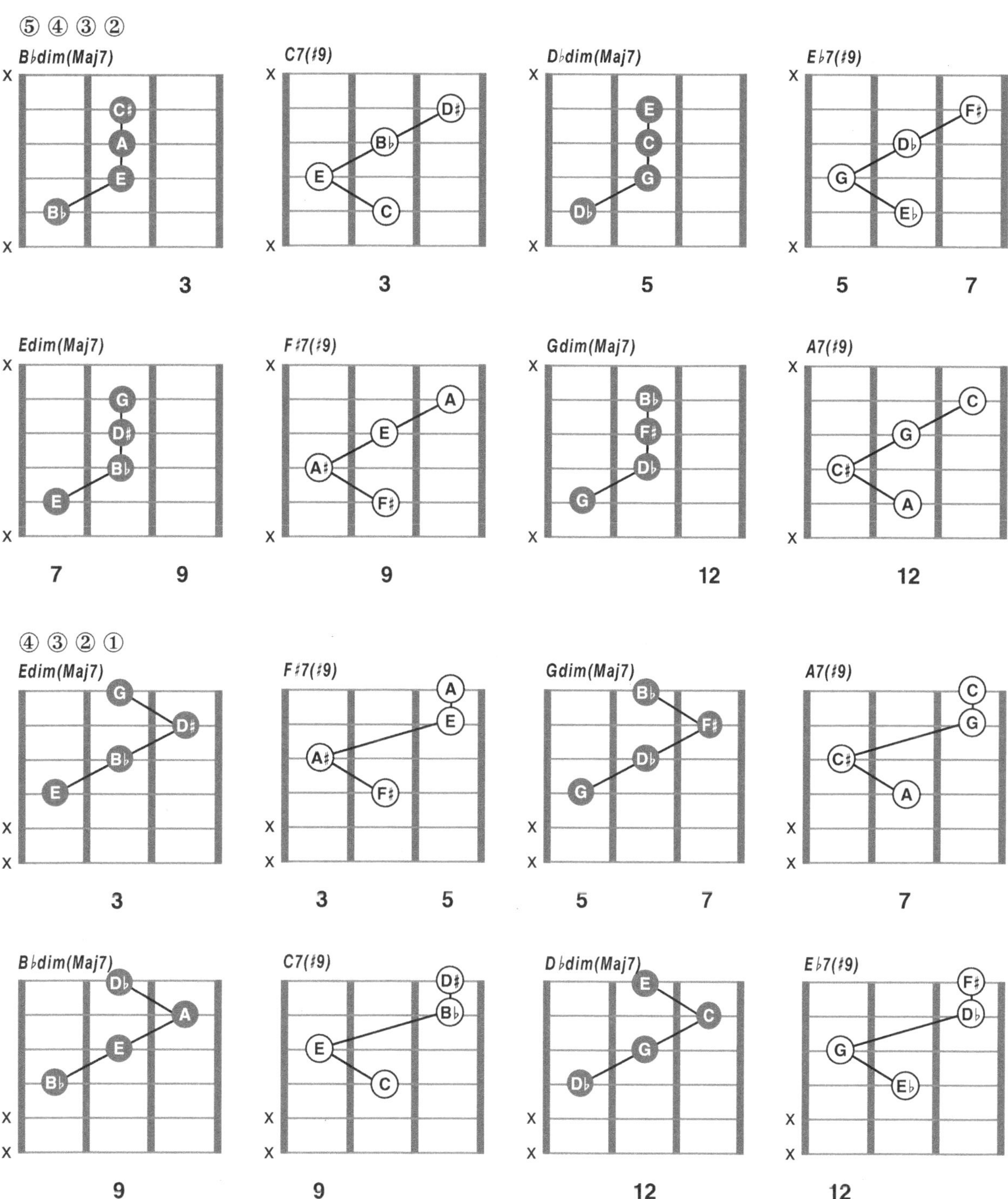

FIG. 14.6. C Symmetrical Diminished (Half/Whole) in Fourths

CHAPTER 15

The Composite Blues Scale and Mixolydian Options

Rhythm and blues, blues, and gospel music involve a fascinating combination of the major pentatonic scale and the blues scale. Here are the notes of the major pentatonic and blues scales from the root G.

FIG. 15.1. G Major Pentatonic and Blues Scales

It's relatively common for electric blues players to alternately play phrases using vocabulary from the blues scale, switching to the major pentatonic for a phrase or two. Combining a cross-section of the two scales, we arrive at what has been described as the *composite blues scale*. Both contain the root and the 5, but the blues scale supplies four more notes, resulting in a nine-note scale.

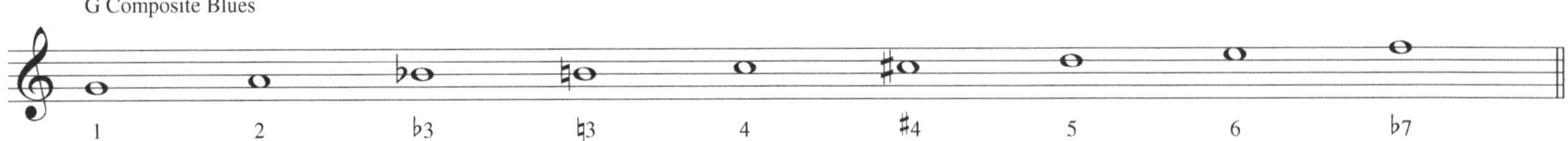

FIG. 15.2. G Composite Blues Scale

In addition to a combination of G major pentatonic and G blues, it also could be seen as G Mixolydian with ♭3 and ♯4 added, or possibly, G Dorian with natural 3 and ♯4 added. Hybrid scales can have many names.

The composite blues scale provides an extraordinary set of harmonic options. Triads, common four-part chords, as well as unusual chords with unusual alterations are made available to us.

Here is a list of options, from each note of the scale:

DEGREE	TRIADS	4-PART CHORDS	TENSIONS
Root	G, Gmin, Gdim	G7, G7sus4, Gmin7, G7♭5, Gdim7	9, ♯9, 11, 13
2	A, Amin	A7, A7sus4, Amin7	♭9, 9, ♯9, 11, ♭13
♭3	B♭, B♭min, B♭dim	B♭Maj7, B♭min(Maj7), B♭dim7, B♭dim(Maj7)	9, ♯9, 11, 13
3	Bdim	Bmin7♭5	♭9, 9, 11, ♭13
4	C	C7, C7sus4, CMaj7	♭9, 9, 11, 13
♯4	C♯dim	C♯dim7, C♯dim(Maj7)	♭9, ♯9, ♭13
5	Dmin	Dmin7, Dmin(Maj7)	9, 11, ♭13, 13
6	Emin, Edim	Emin7♭5, Edim7	♭9, 11, ♭13, 13
♭7	F, Faug	FMaj7, FMaj7♯5	9, 11, ♯11, 13

FIG. 15.3. Composite Blues Scale and Its Harmonies

Over a one-chord vamp, guitarists can mix and match the voicings made available by this scale. It's mostly a matter of *tension* (away from the tonic) to *release* (back home to the tonic). Here's an example, demonstrating notes from the G composite blues scale. It's inspired by the great gospel pianist/performer Billy Preston.

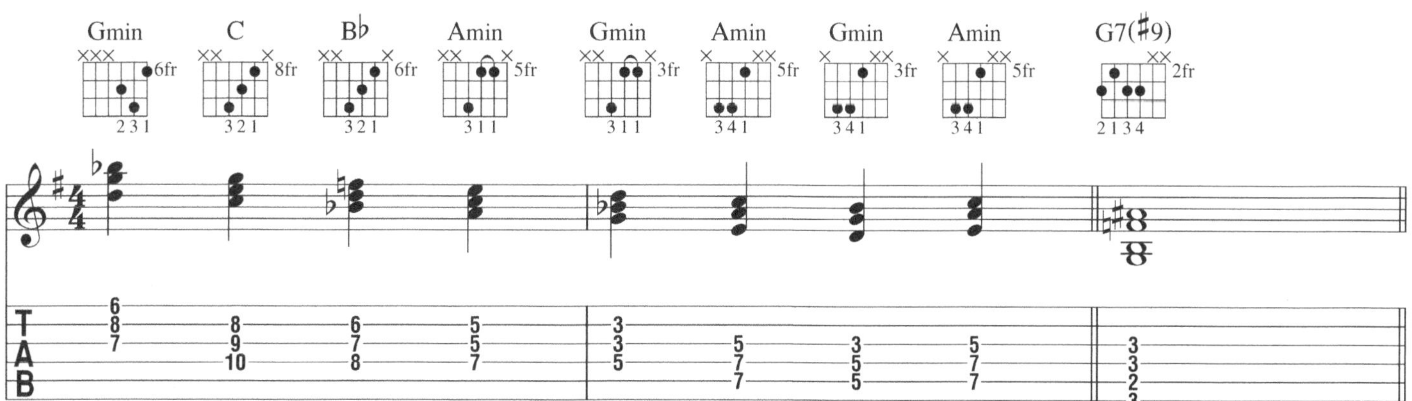

FIG.15.4. G Composite Blues Example

It can be easier to think of harmonic ideas while thinking about the Mixolydian scale, mixed with the blues scale. These voicings can be used over an extended period of G major, G7, G minor, or Gmin7 harmony.

G Mixolydian
G Amin Bdim C Dmin Emin F
G Blues-Derived Chords
Gmin Gdim B♭min B♭

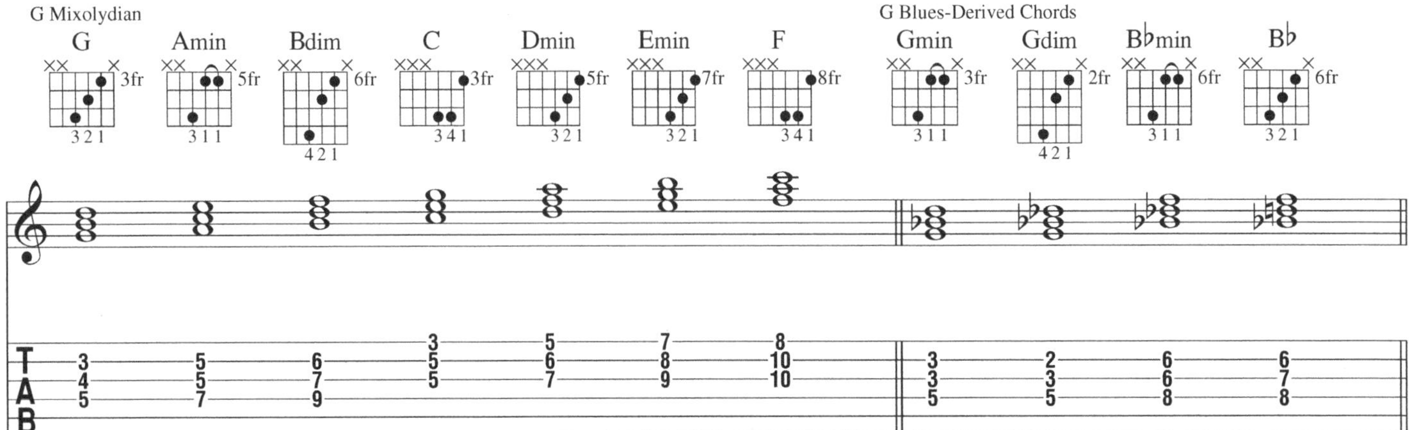

FIG. 15.5. Chords Derived from G Mixolydian and G Blues

Here is an etude, demonstrating a quick trip through many of the available triads, provided by the composite blues scale. Play through the written voicings, then improvise using the available triads shown in figure 15.6. Feel free to vary the inversions that you use (primarily emphasizing the higher pitched strings), and use longer and shorter rhythmic durations to explore the harmony in a musical way.

23, 24

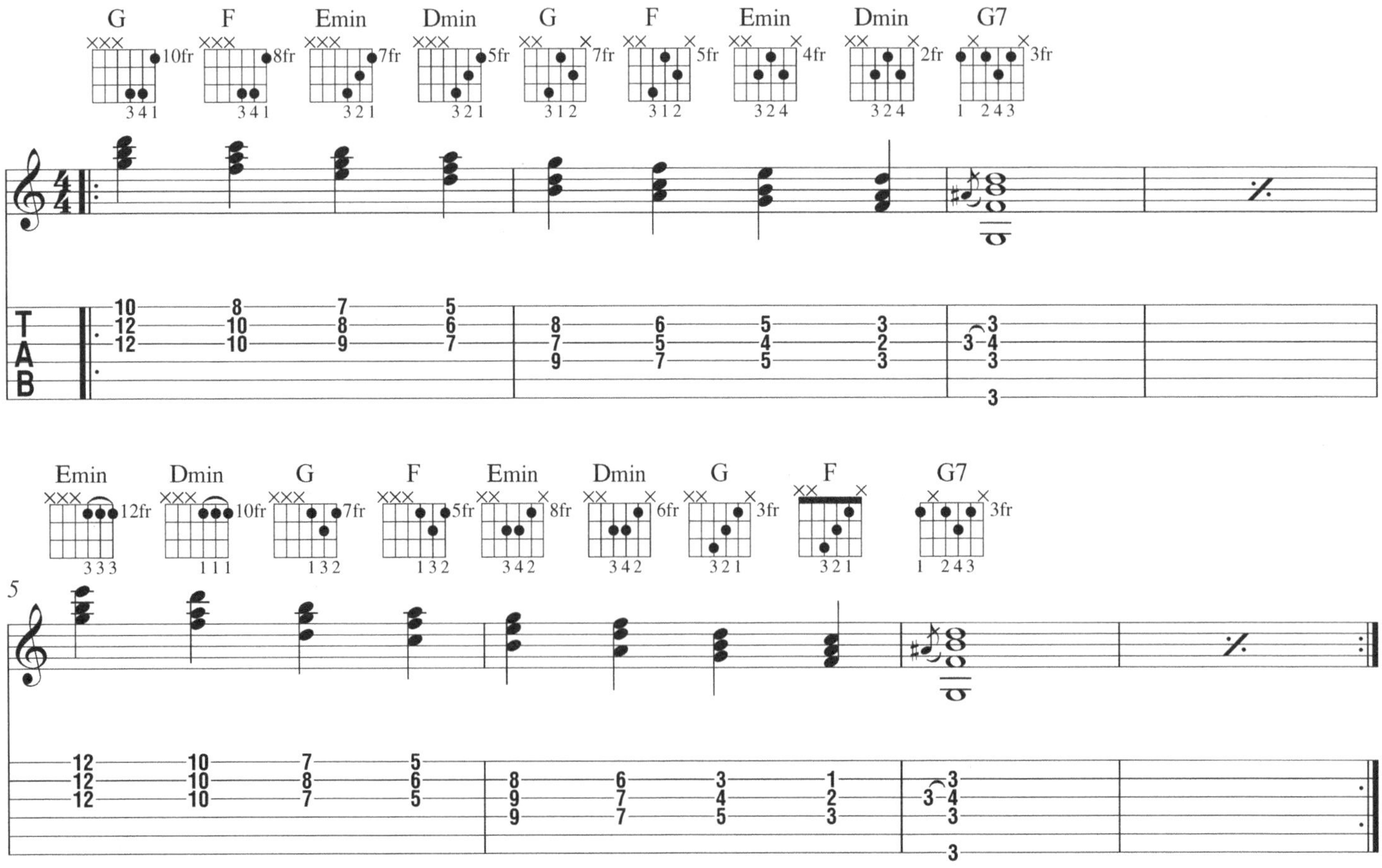

G F Emin Dmin G F Emin Dmin G7
Emin Dmin G F Emin Dmin G F G7

FIG. 15.6. Composite Blues Scale Etude

Here are the available colors for your improvised harmonic performance, as provided by the composite blues scale.

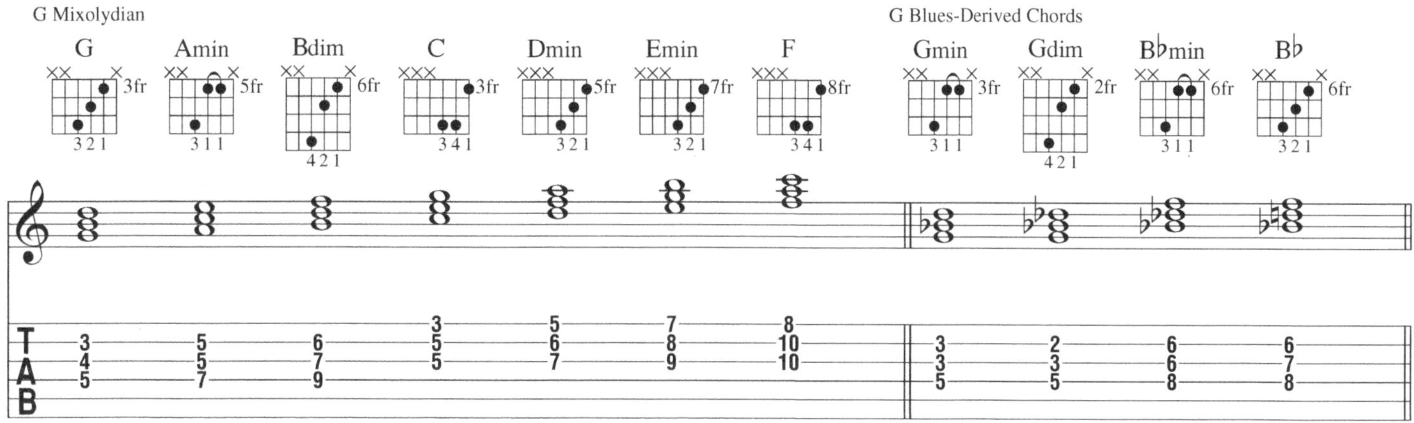

FIG. 15.7. G Composite Blues Scale Sample Harmony

CHAPTER 16

Modal Voicings on Standard Progressions

Using modal sounds for harmonic accompaniment for many guitarists is often relegated to extended jams involving one chord. It's more than possible to "shift gears" harmonically in chord progressions found in standard progressions. It takes a lot of concentration at first, but if you are able to identify a chord scale for a given chord, or a single chord scale that applies to a set of chords in a progression, modal voicings can sound fresh and modern. This approach truly opens the door into using modal harmony to its fullest extent.

See the following etudes for ideas to do similar treatments to the following standard progressions. "The World's Most Common Jazz Bossa Progression" and "Common Fall-Time Progression" are the most frequently popular selections I've heard from students. The harmonic shifts in "Tribute to Dave's Sweet Way Progression" will put you through several tonicized areas. "Time for Contemplating Progression" is reminiscent of the music of McCoy Tyner, as found on *The Real McCoy,* from 1967. "R&B/Pop Song Progression" takes an often-performed pop progression and puts it through some interesting modal colors.

Use the concept of *playing across the scales* modally to enhance your comping and harmonic choices on standard progressions. Expand your harmonic horizons beyond single-chord vamps! Play through the notated selections with the demonstration tracks, then venture forth with your own variations with the backing tracks provided.

25, 26

The World's Most Common Jazz Bossa Progression

Cmin7 Cmin7 Fmin7 Fmin7

Dmin7♭5 G7(alt) Cmin7 Cmin7

E♭min7 A♭7 D♭Maj7 D♭Maj7

Dmin7♭5 G7(alt) Cmin7 G7(alt) Cmin7

FIG. 16.1. The World's Most Common Jazz Bossa Progression

Common Fall-Time Progression

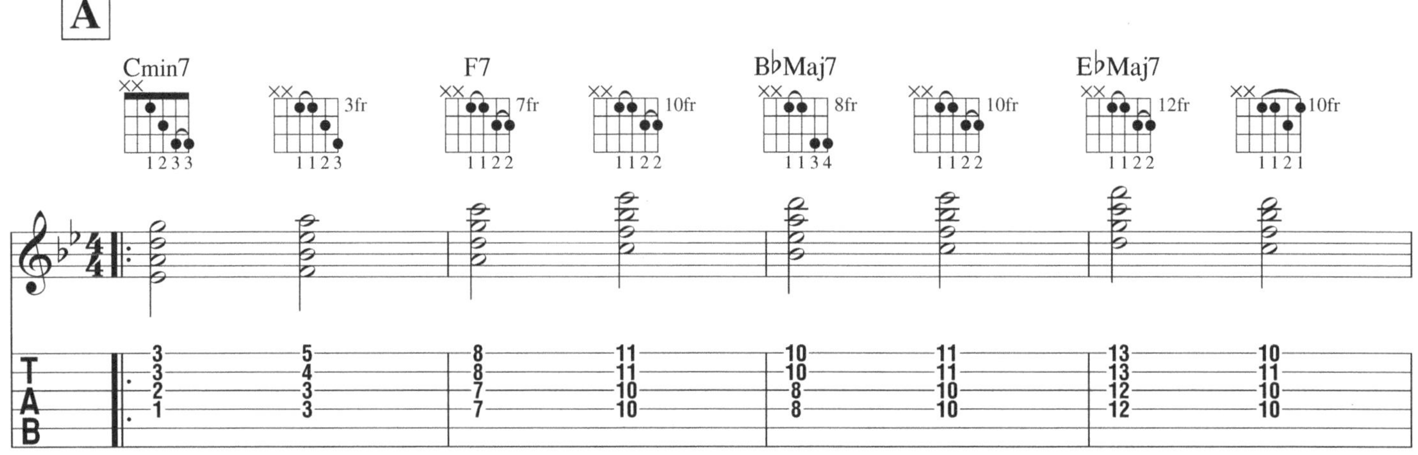

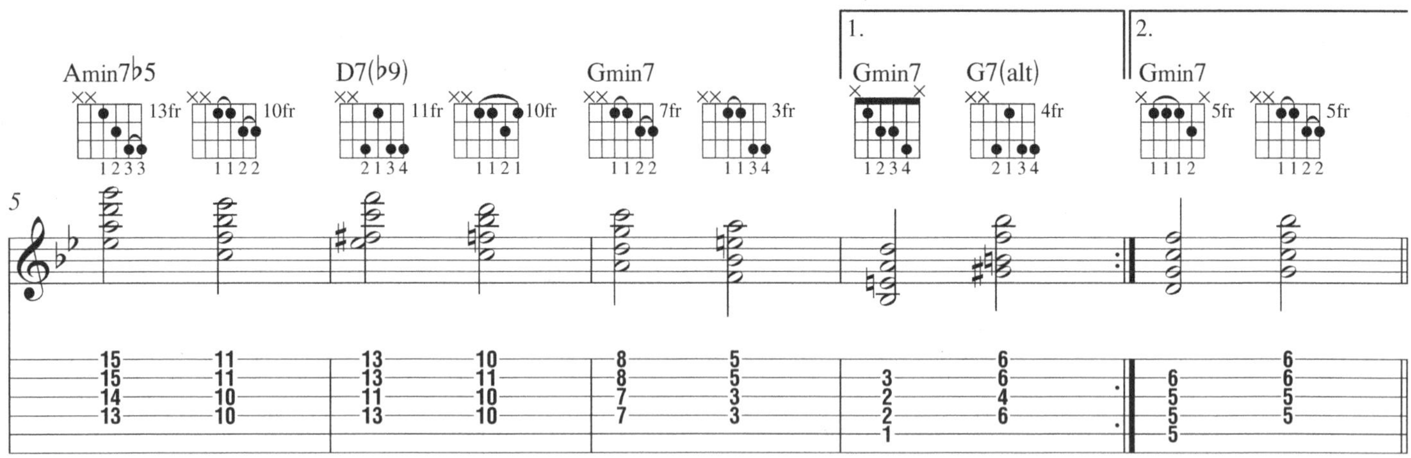

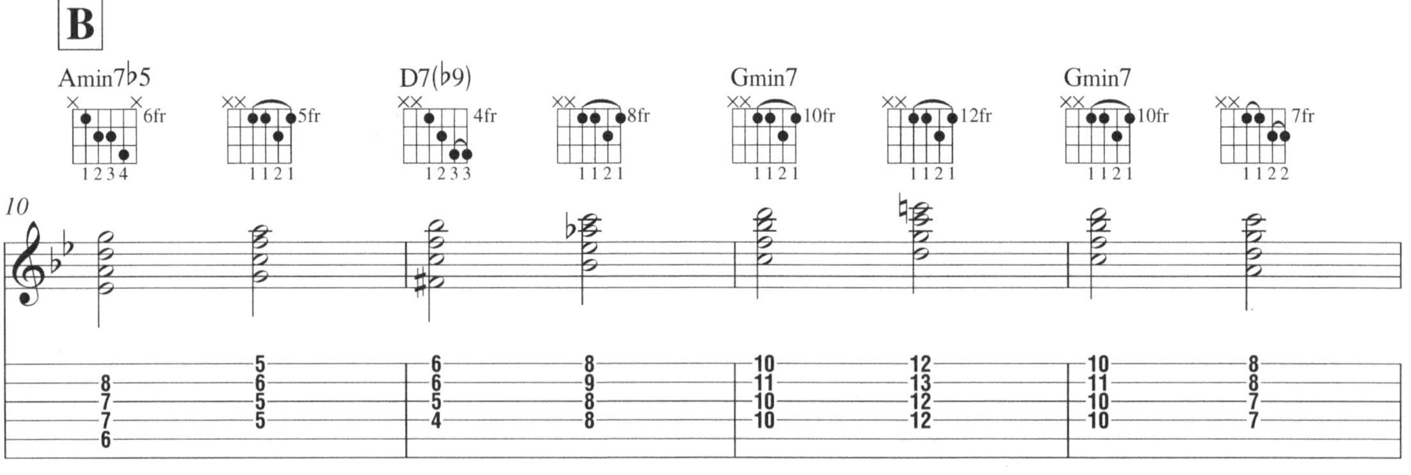

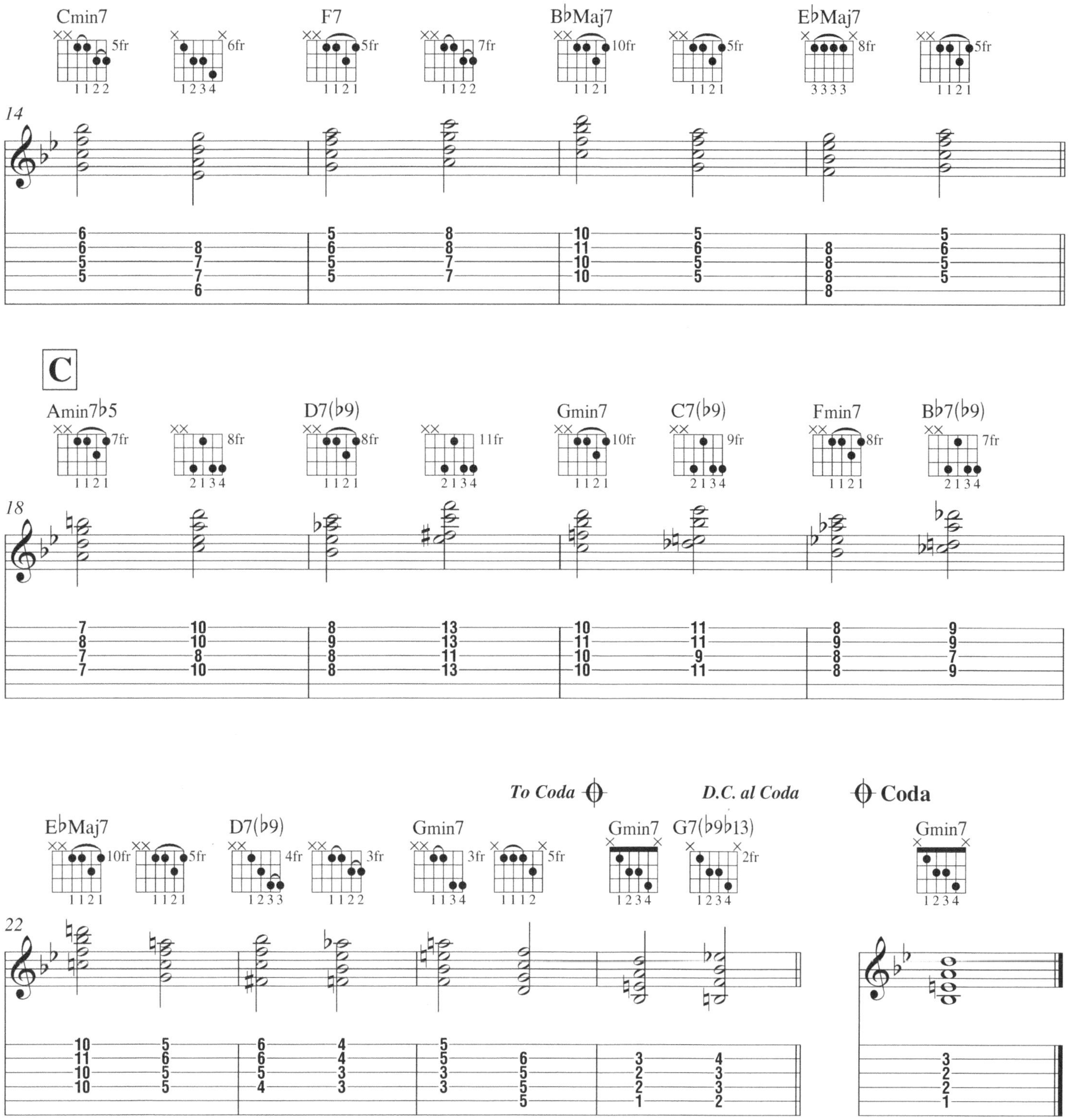

Cmin7 F7 B♭Maj7 E♭Maj7

14

C

Amin7♭5 D7(♭9) Gmin7 C7(♭9) Fmin7 B♭7(♭9)

18

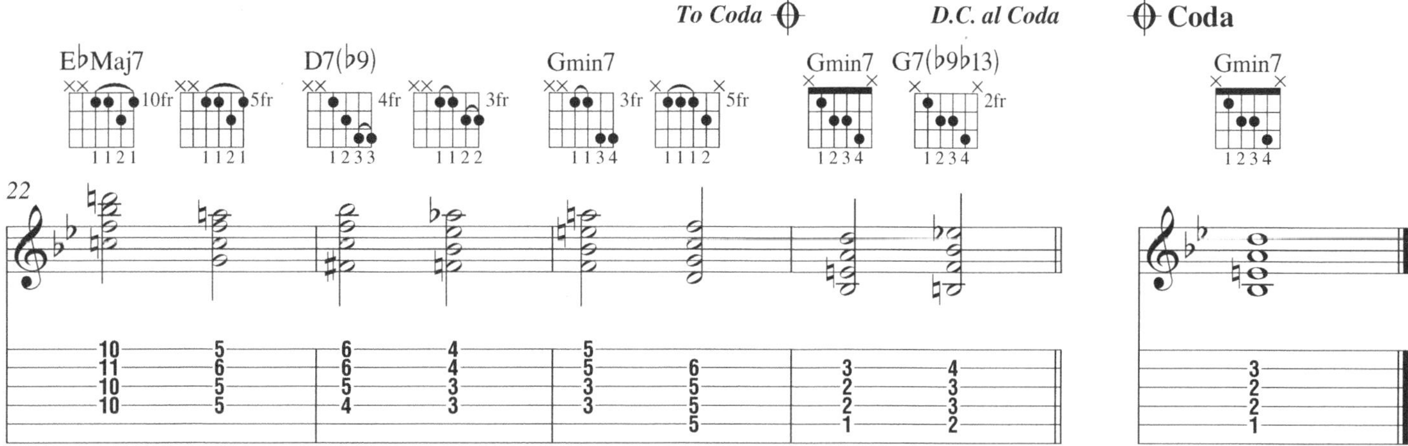

FIG. 16.2. Common Fall-Time Progression

29, 30

Tribute to Dave's Sweet Way Progression

Amin7♭5 6fr D7(♭9) 4fr Gmin7 5fr C7 8fr Cmin7 5fr F7 6fr B♭7 5fr E♭Maj7 5fr

5 A♭min7 6fr D♭7 8fr G♭Maj7 6fr BMaj7 6fr Cmin7♭5 4fr F7 6fr 1. B♭Maj7 5fr 5fr 2. B♭Maj7♭5 7fr 7fr

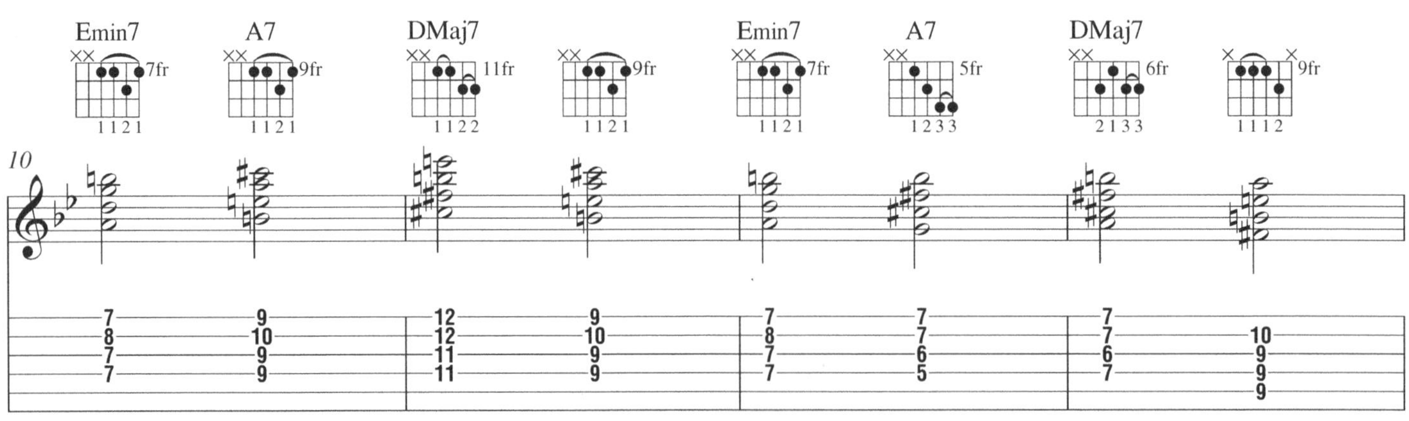

Dmin7
G7
CMaj7
E♭7
E♭min7
A♭7
Dmin7
G7
Amin7♭5
D7(♭9)
Gmin7
C7
Cmin7
F7
B♭7
E♭Maj7
A♭min7
D♭7
G♭Maj7
BMaj7
Cmin7♭5
F7
B♭Maj7

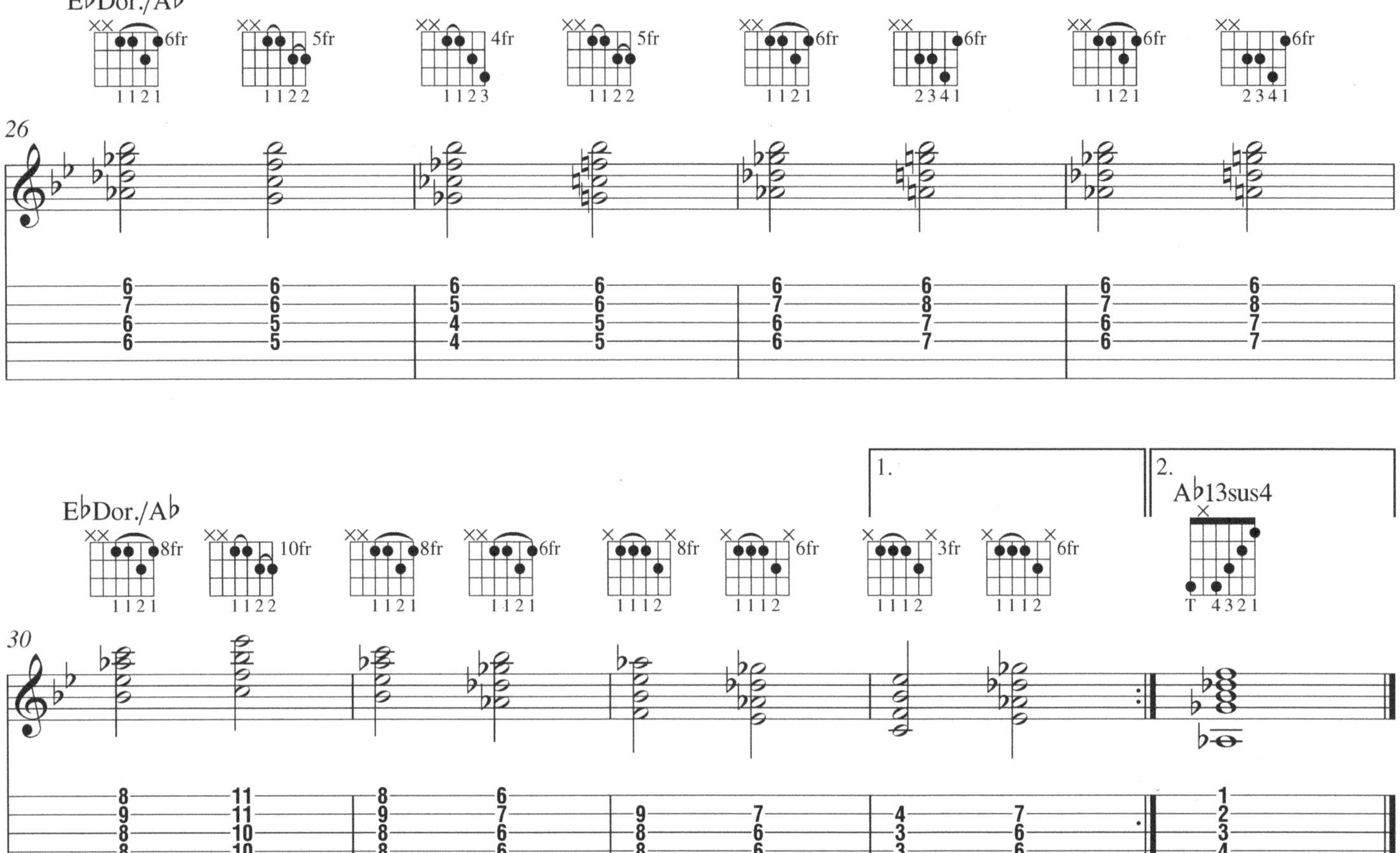

FIG. 16.3. Tribute to Dave's Sweet Way Progression

31, 32

Time for Contemplating Progression

Cmin7: C Dorian

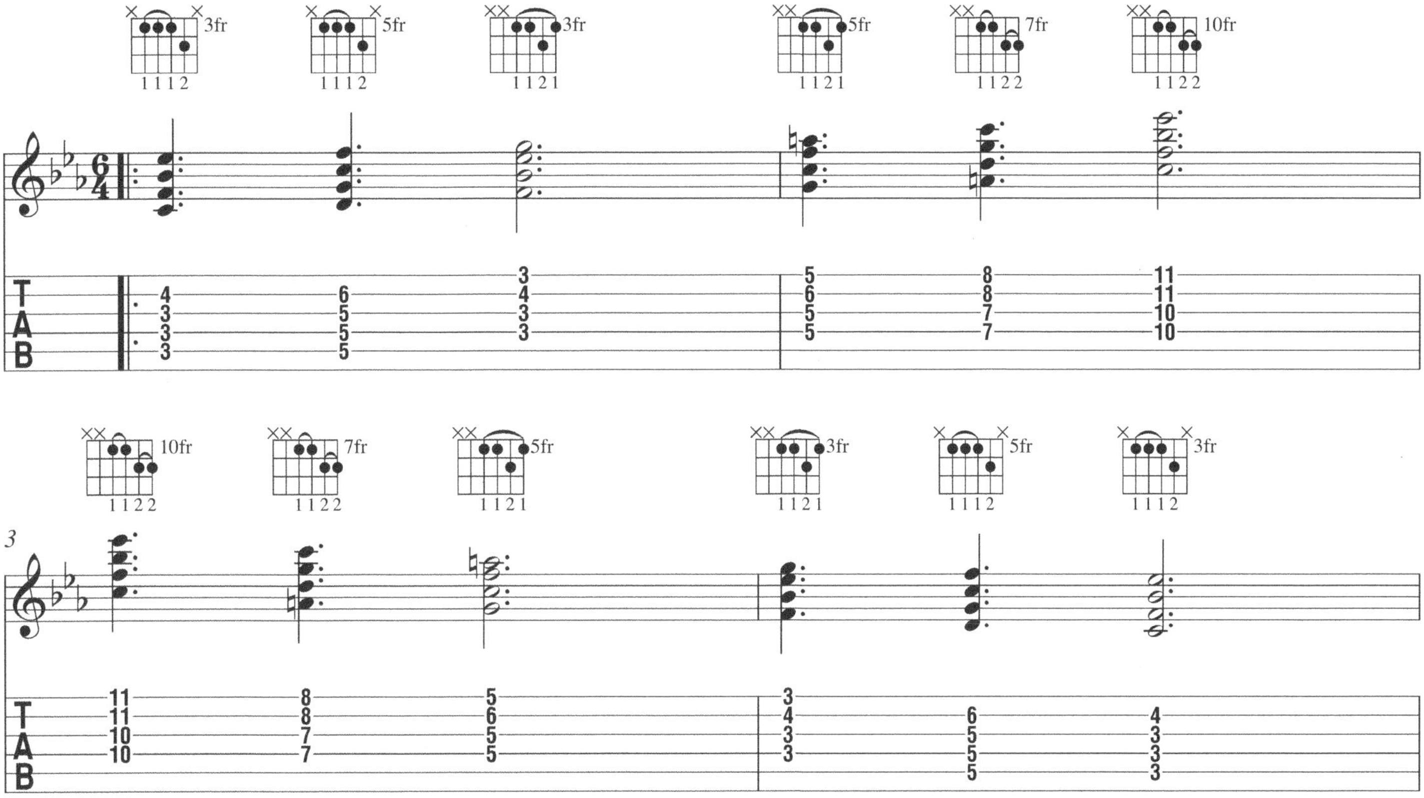

AbMaj7(#11): Ab Lydian = F Dorian

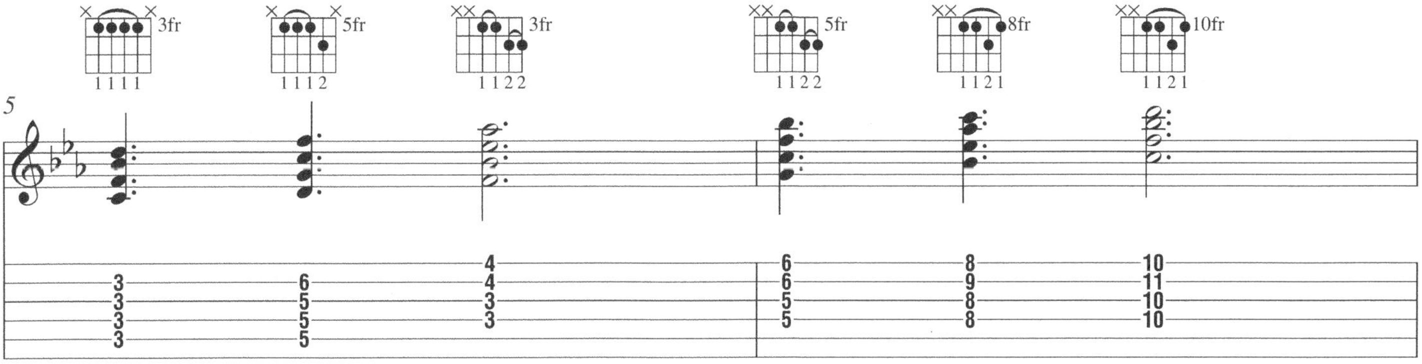

G(alt): G Altered

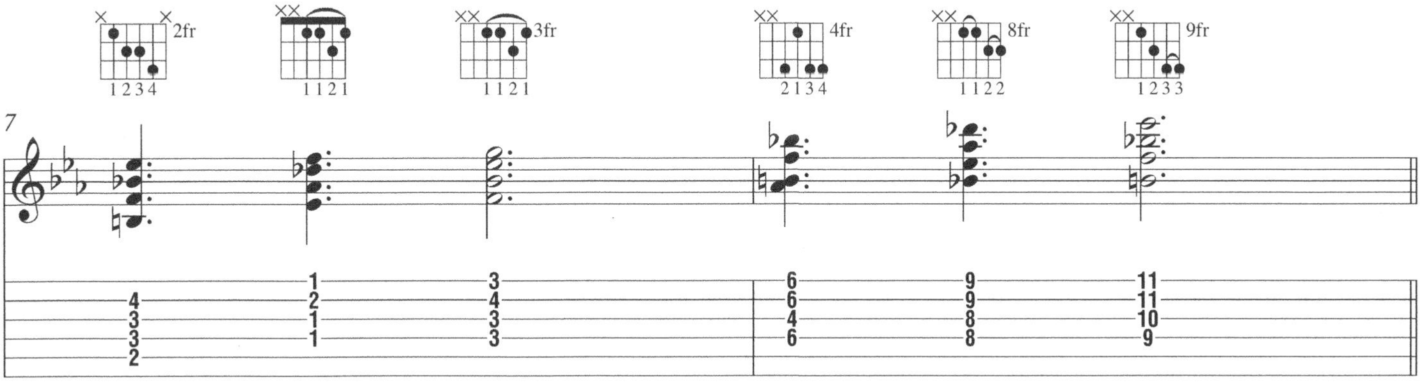

FIG. 16.4. Time for Contemplating Progression

33, 34

R&B/Pop Song Progression

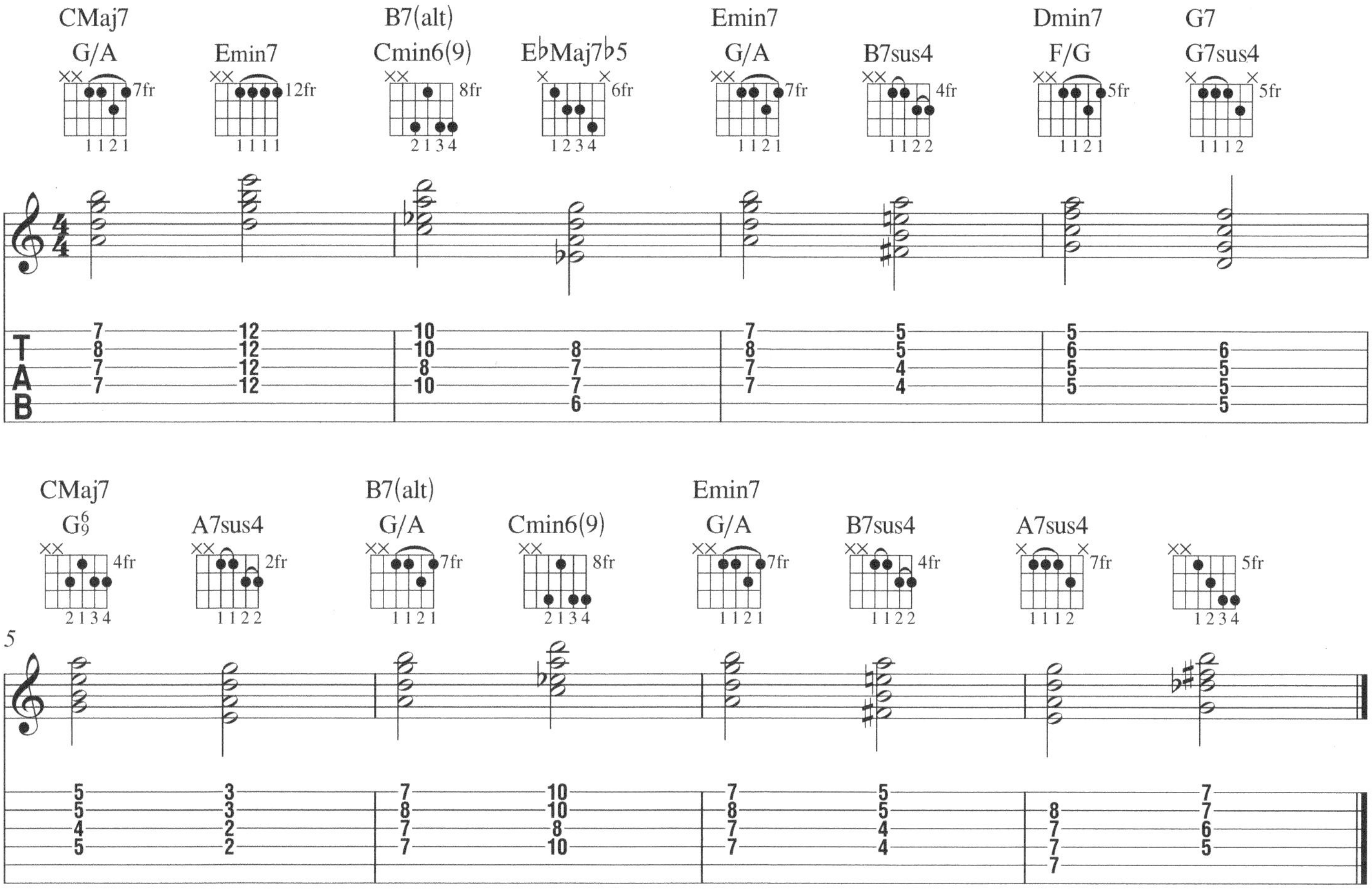

Chord	Voicing	Position	Fingering	Tab (strings 1–6)
CMaj7	G/A	7fr	1 1 2 1	7, 8, 7, 7, –, –
	Emin7	12fr	1 1 1 1	12, 12, 12, 12, –, –
B7(alt)	Cmin6(9)	8fr	2 1 3 4	10, 10, 8, 10, –, –
	E♭Maj7♭5	6fr	1 2 3 4	–, 8, 7, 7, 6, –
Emin7	G/A	7fr	1 1 2 1	7, 8, 7, 7, –, –
	B7sus4	4fr	1 1 2 2	5, 5, 4, 4, –, –
Dmin7	F/G	5fr	1 1 2 1	5, 6, 5, 5, –, –
G7	G7sus4	5fr	1 1 1 2	–, 6, 5, 5, 5, –

5

Chord	Voicing	Position	Fingering	Tab (strings 1–6)
CMaj7	G6/9	4fr	2 1 3 4	5, 5, 4, 5, –, –
	A7sus4	2fr	1 1 2 2	3, 3, 2, 2, –, –
B7(alt)	G/A	7fr	1 1 2 1	7, 8, 7, 7, –, –
	Cmin6(9)	8fr	2 1 3 4	10, 10, 8, 10, –, –
Emin7	G/A	7fr	1 1 2 1	7, 8, 7, 7, –, –
	B7sus4	4fr	1 1 2 2	5, 5, 4, 4, –, –
	A7sus4	7fr	1 1 1 2	–, 8, 7, 7, 7, –
		5fr	1 2 3 4	7, 7, 6, 5, –, –

FIG. 16.5. R&B/Pop Song Progression

APPENDIX A

Great "Pianoless Trio" Jazz Recordings for Practicing Chordal Accompaniment

To get great comping practice, import any track from the following recordings into your recording software. Add a guitar track, overdubbing your own comping. Work to integrate your accompaniment with the recorded performance.

Ensure that your playing fits well rhythmically with the drummer's performance. Consider the composition's chord changes, complement the soloist and pay attention to the chords implied by the bassist's lines.

The comper is responsible to support:

1. The soloist.
2. The composition, meaning the form and its double bars.
3. The rhythm section, meaning drums (primarily) and the bassist.
4. The listener's perspective. Considering the overall sound of the moment, is a little accompaniment needed, or a lot?

If it's a song you don't know, try to learn it from the recording. Find the recordings and play along! If it's a song you already know, do your best to integrate your playing with the great performance. Record yourself in performance along with the track, and evaluate the result.

If that's too difficult, locate a lead sheet for the song in question using a fakebook or online resource. Remember, a lead sheet often serves as a rough outline for the chords played on a standard. Work to learn new substitute chords from the masters, using your ear. Use your ear to figure out appropriate accompaniment; work to achieve balance.

When listening to the recording of your comping along with the track, keep these thoughts in mind:

1. What's good about what you're doing?
2. What's in need of improvement?
3. What are you going to do to gain the improvement you need?

These are all great recordings for comping practice:

Sonny Rollins

Way Out West, Contemporary, 1957
A Night at the Village Vanguard, Blue Note, 1958

John Coltrane

Lush Life (first three tracks), Prestige, 1961
Impressions ("Impressions" from 2:30 on) Prestige, 1963
Both Directions ("Impressions" Take 3 and Take 4), Verve, recorded in 1963, released in 2018.

Grant Green

Standards, Blue Note, recorded in 1961

Lee Konitz

Motion, Verve, 1961

Chet Baker and Lee Konitz

In Concert, India Navigation, recorded in 1974

Joe Henderson

State of the Tenor, Blue Note, 1986
The Standard Joe, Red Records, 1991

Dave Holland Trio

Triplicate, ECM, 1988

Charlie Haden

The Montreal Tapes: Tribute to Joe Henderson, Verve, 1989

Kenny Garrett

Triology, Warner Brothers, 1995

Walter Smith III

Twio, Walter Smith III, 2018

APPENDIX B

Voicing Compendium

Practice the following etudes by playing the given voicings in your own rhythm and order, ascending and descending. The audio tracks have sample guitar performances, in varying levels of complexity, but you should develop your own ideas.

35, 36

Dorian Voicings in Twelve Keys

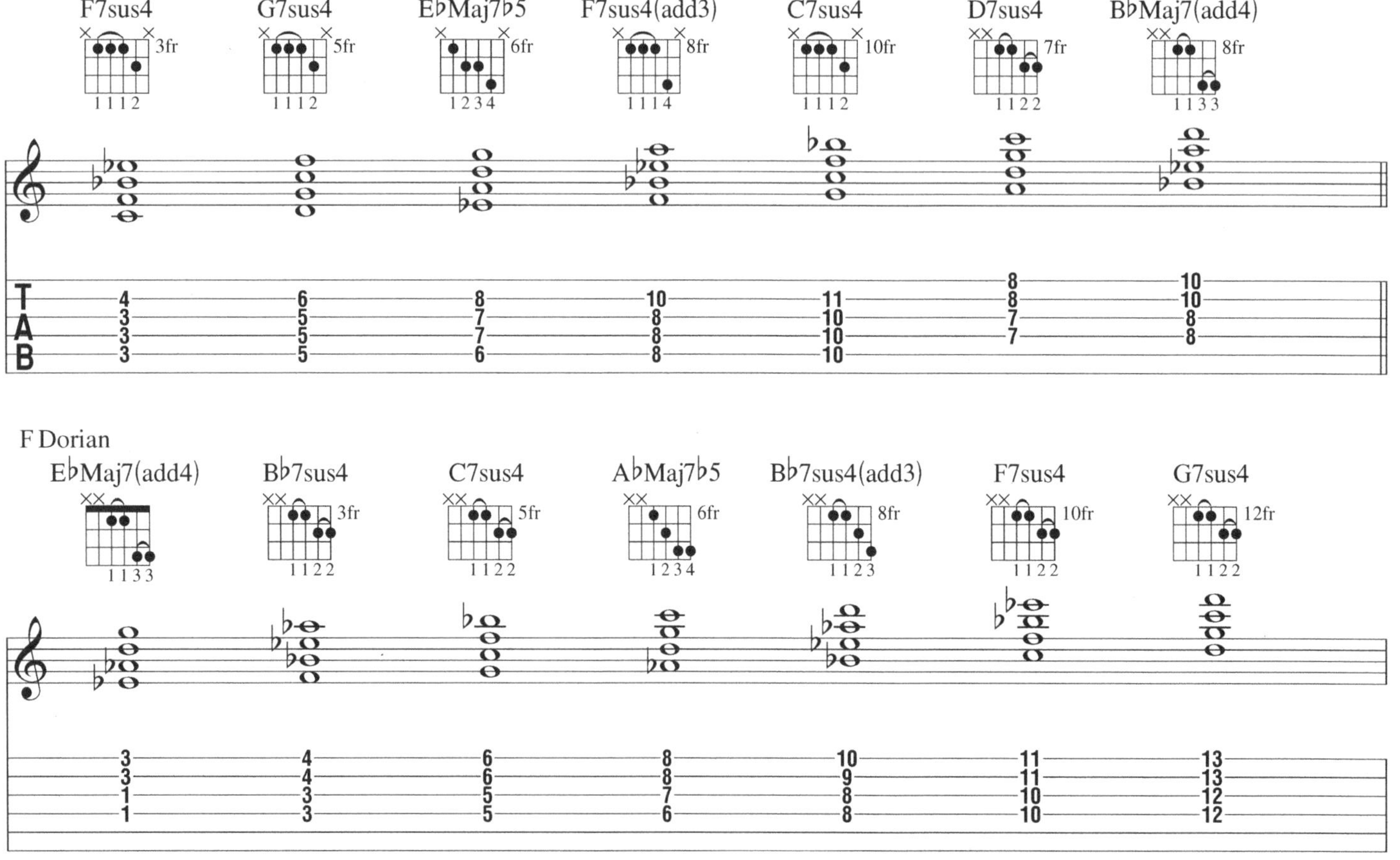

B♭ Dorian
E♭7sus4
F7sus4
D♭Maj7♭5
E♭7sus4(add3)
B♭7sus4
C7sus4
A♭Maj7(add4)
E♭ Dorian
A♭7sus4
B♭7sus4
G♭Maj7♭5
A♭7sus4(add3)
E♭7sus4
F7sus4
D♭Maj7(add4)
A♭ Dorian
A♭7sus4
B♭7sus4
G♭Maj7(add4)
D♭7sus4
E♭7sus4
BMaj7♭5
D♭7sus4(add3)
D♭ Dorian
G♭7sus4
A♭7sus4
F♭Maj7♭5
G♭7sus4(add3)
D♭7sus4
E♭7sus4
B♭Maj7(add4)

F♯ Dorian
F♯7sus4
G♯7sus4
EMaj7(add4)
B7sus4
C♯7sus4
AMaj7♭5
B7sus4(add3)
B Dorian
E7sus4
F♯7sus4
DMaj7♭5
E7sus4(add3)
B7sus4
C♯7sus4
AMaj7(add4)
E Dorian
A7sus4
B7sus4
GMaj7♭5
A7sus4(add3)
E7sus4
F♯7sus4
DMaj7(add4)

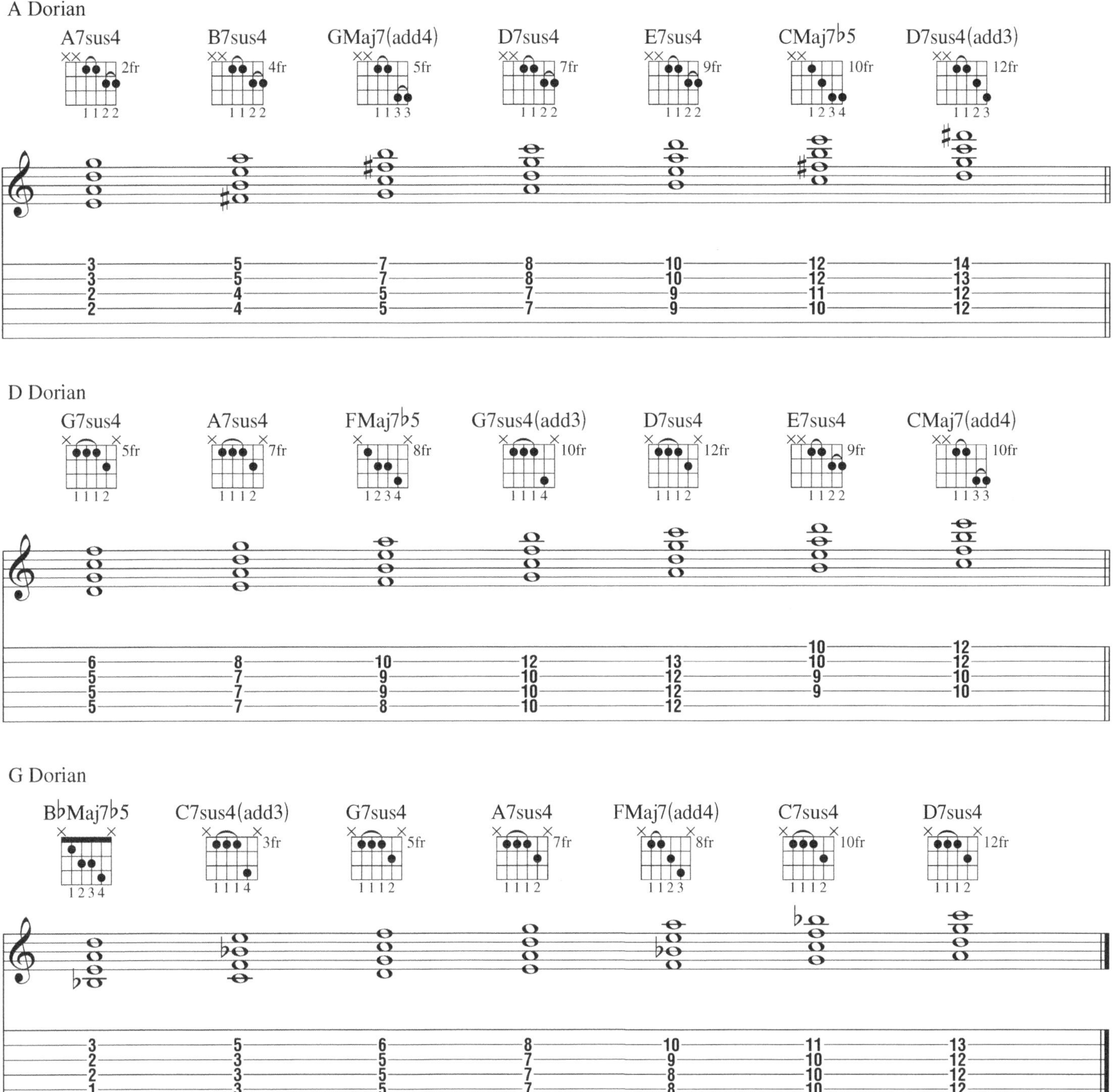

FIG. B.1. Dorian Voicings in Twelve Keys

37, 38

Quartal Voicings in Nine Colors

Cmin6(9)

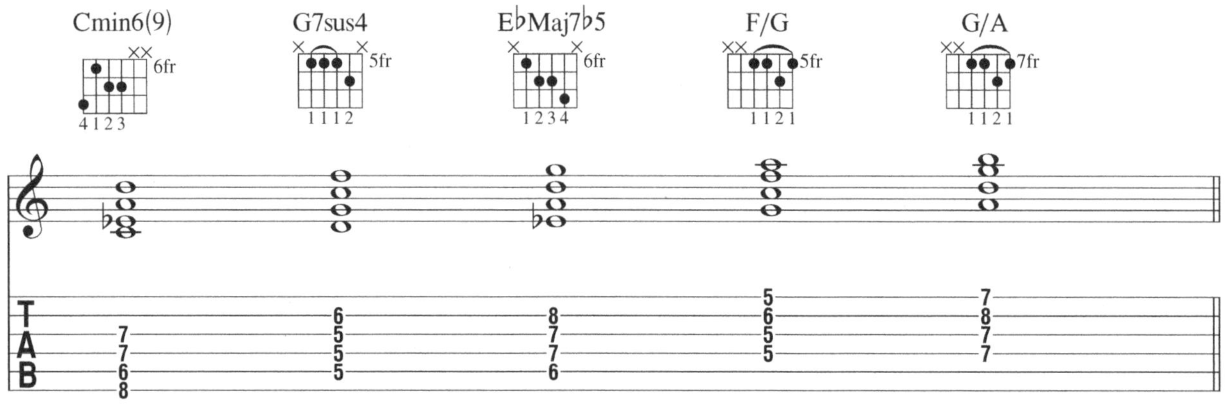

Cmin6(9) 6fr 4123 | G7sus4 5fr 1112 | E♭Maj7♭5 6fr 1234 | F/G 5fr 1121 | G/A 7fr 1121

Cmin7

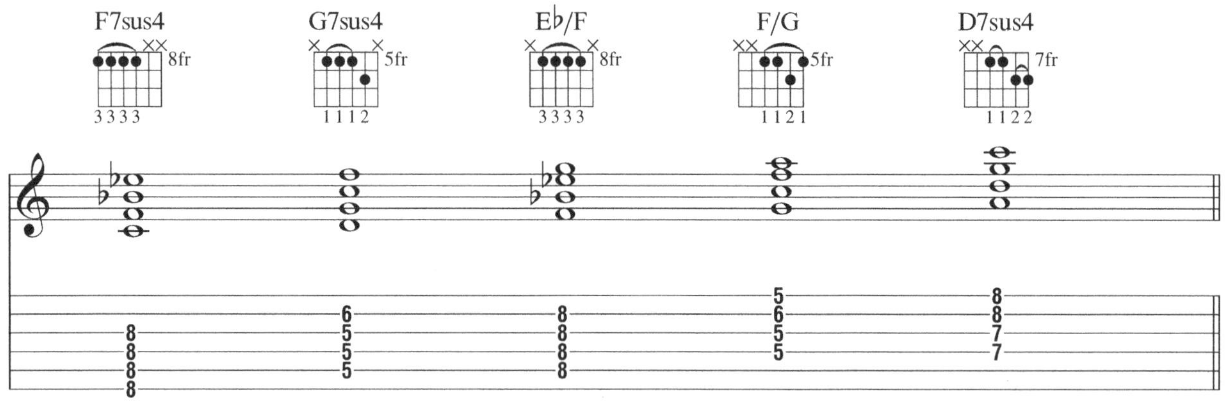

F7sus4 8fr 3333 | G7sus4 5fr 1112 | E♭/F 8fr 3333 | F/G 5fr 1121 | D7sus4 7fr 1122

Cmin7♭5

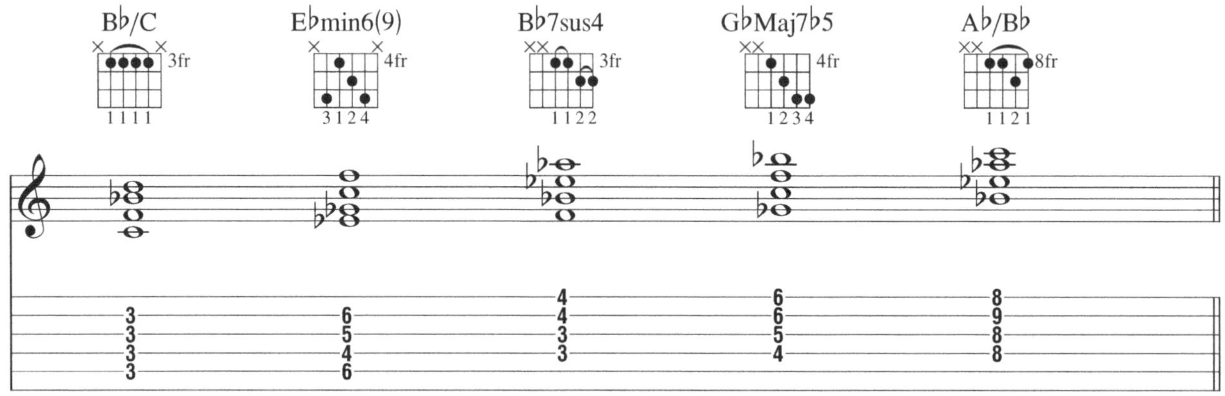

B♭/C 3fr 1111 | E♭min6(9) 4fr 3124 | B♭7sus4 3fr 1122 | G♭Maj7♭5 4fr 1234 | A♭/B♭ 8fr 1121

CMaj7
A7sus4
7fr
1 1 1 3
G6(9)
9fr
2 1 1 3
G/A
7fr
1 1 2 1
E7sus4
9fr
1 1 2 2
Em/D
12fr
3 3 3 3
C7sus4
B♭/C
3fr
1 1 1 1
G7sus4
5fr
1 1 1 2
A7sus4
7fr
3 3 3 4
C7sus4
5fr
1 1 2 2
D7sus4
7fr
1 1 2 2
C7(9,♯11)
C/D
5fr
1 1 1 1
D/E
7fr
1 1 1 1
Gmin6(9)
8fr
3 1 2 4
D7sus4
7fr
1 1 2 2
B♭Maj7♭5
8fr
1 2 3 4

FIG. B.2. Quartal Voicings in Nine Colors

APPENDIX C

Practice Tracks for Fluency in Twelve Keys

Six of the most prevalent chordal structures are presented here in all twelve keys, ordered in the circle of fourths. Listen to the guitar demo tracks, but, most of all, play through the voicing types with the recorded backing tracks, presented in this book in all keys. Go beyond rote performance to achieve great rhythmic feel and flow. For minor 7 voicing content, refer to chapter 2 and appendix B.

39 – 42

Minor 7

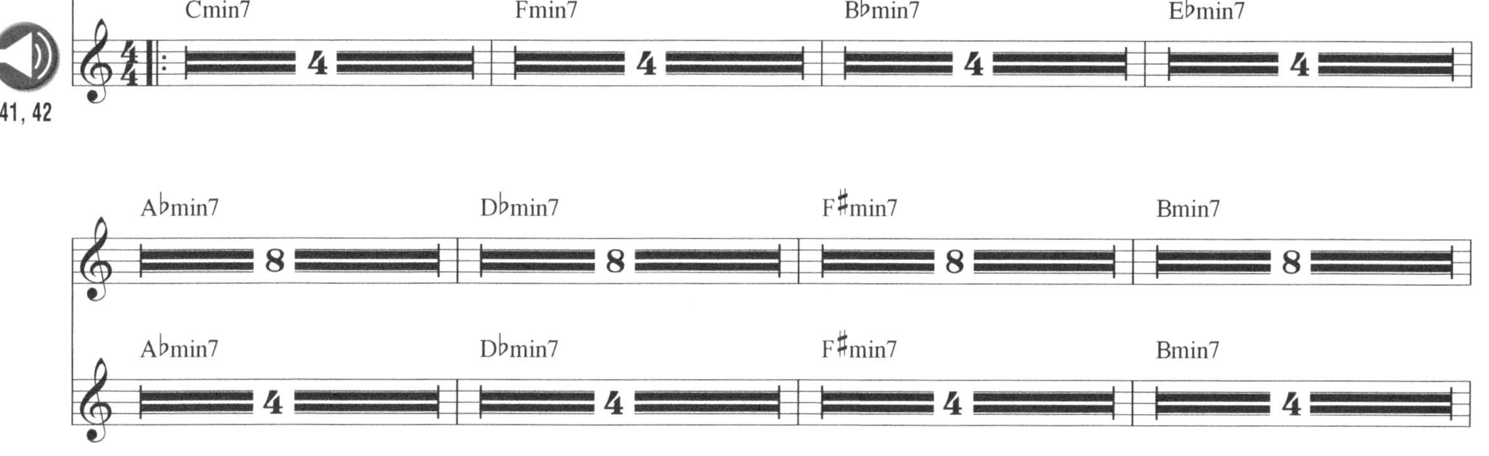

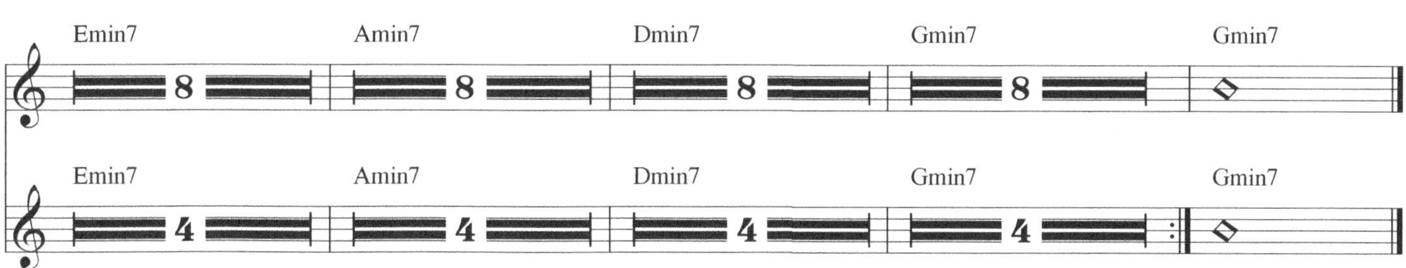

FIG. C.1. Minor 7: Eight Bars, Four Bars

Refer to chapter 7 (page 24).

Dominant 7

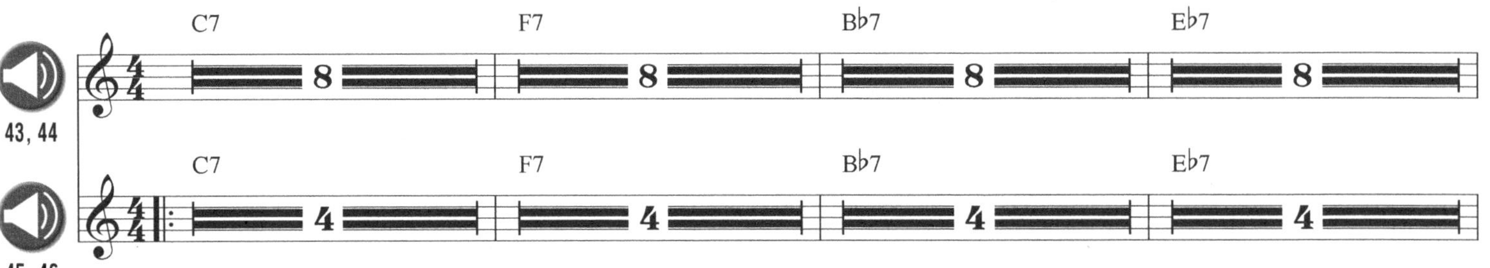

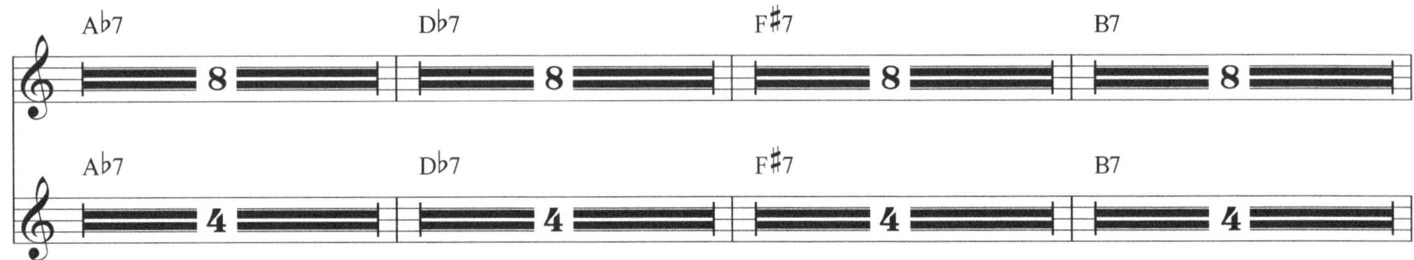

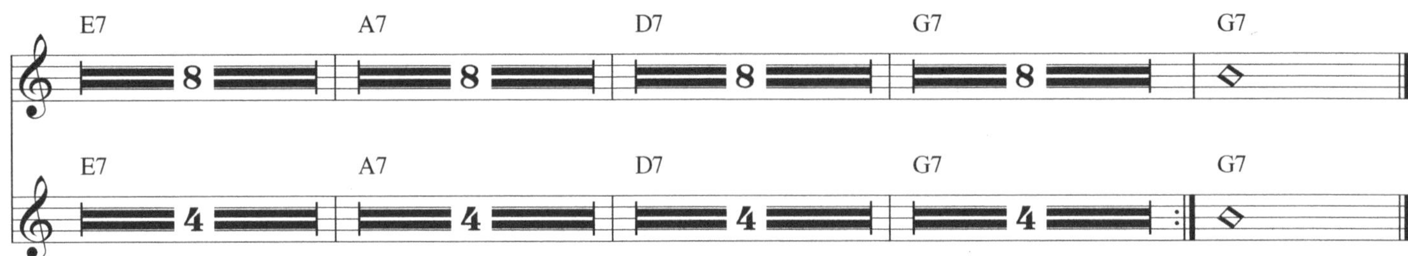

FIG. C.2. Dominant 7: Eight Bars, Four Bars

Refer to chapter 8 (page 28).

Altered 7

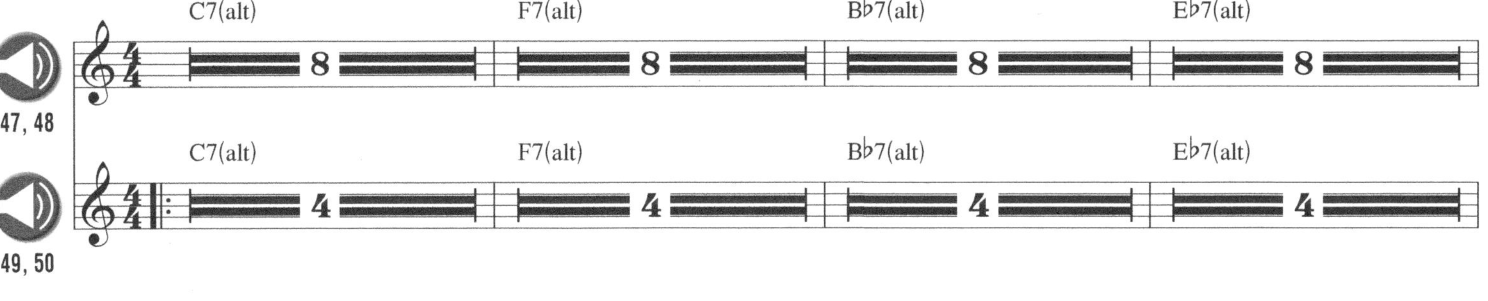

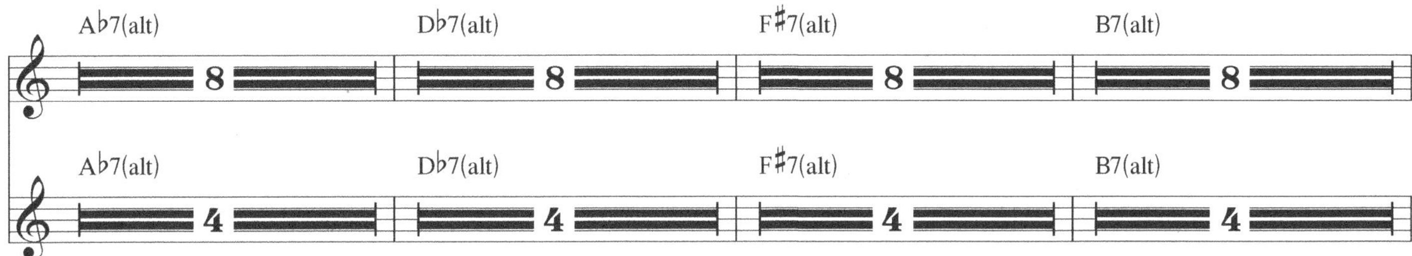

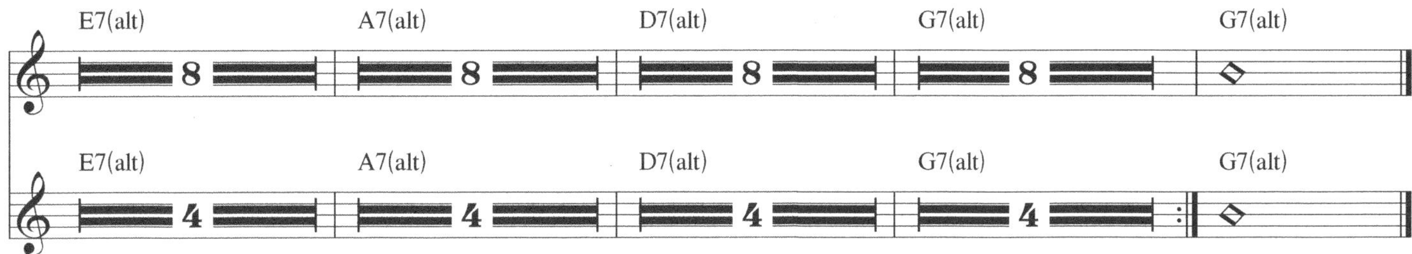

FIG. C.3. Altered 7: Eight Bars, Four Bars

Refer to chapter 11 (page 44).

51 – 54

Minor 7♭5

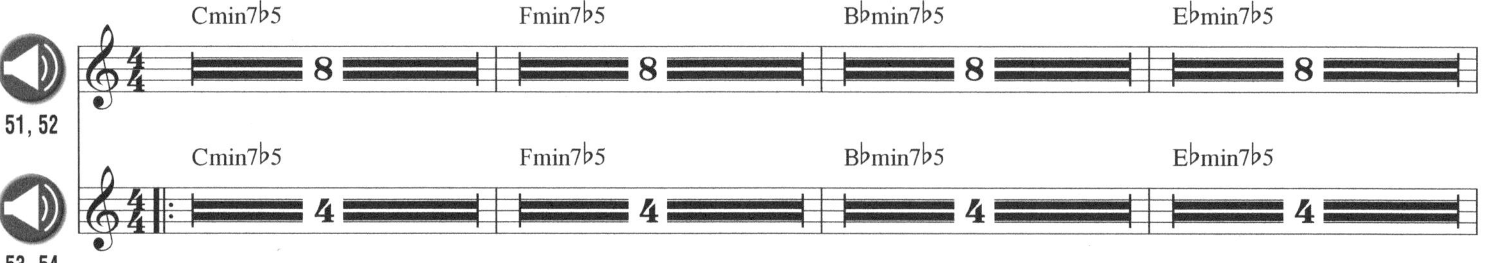

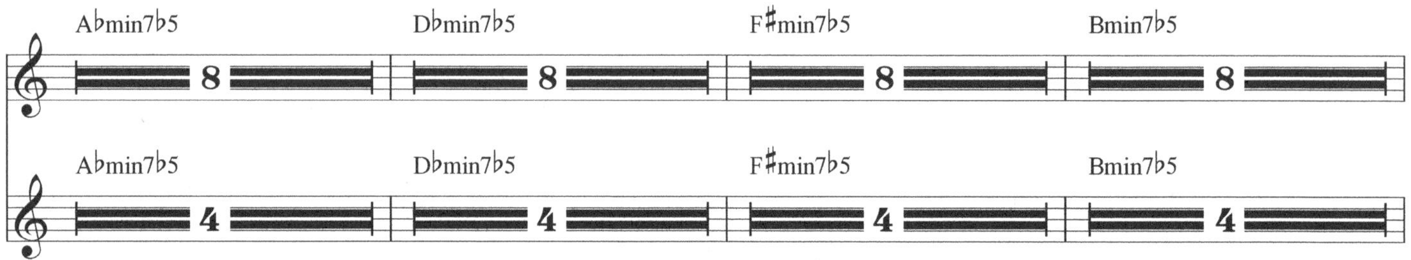

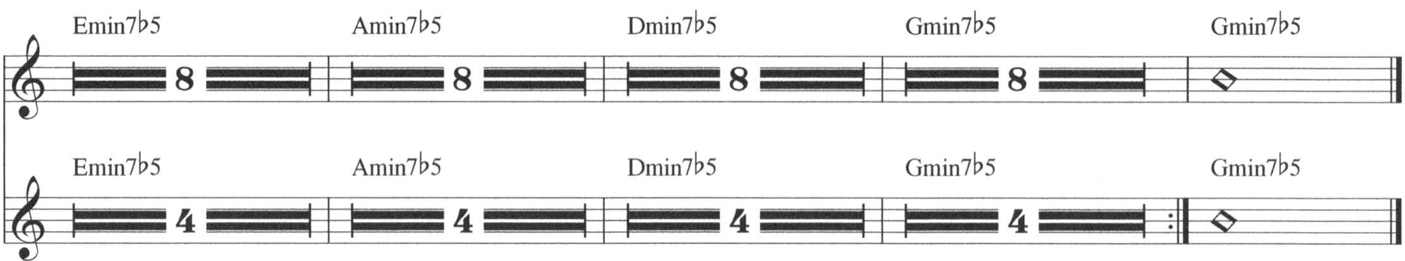

FIG. C.4. Minor 7♭5: Eight Bars, Four Bars

Refer to chapter 12 (page 50).

Major 7

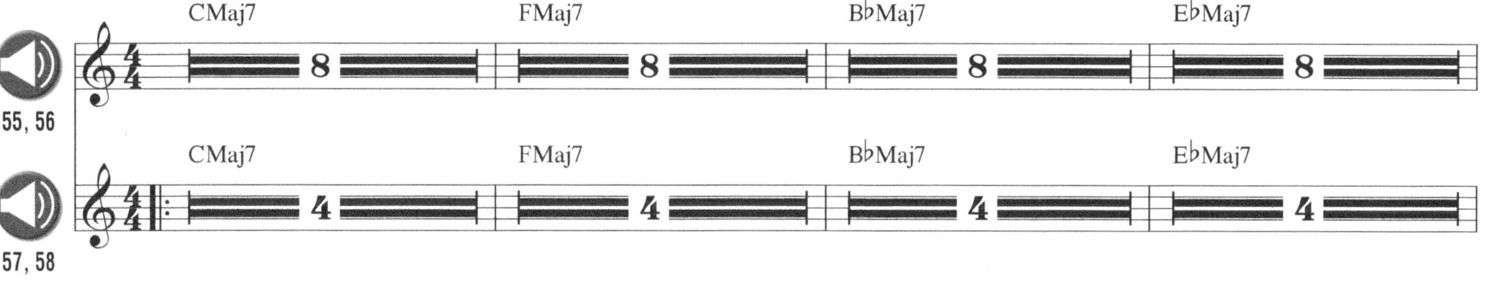

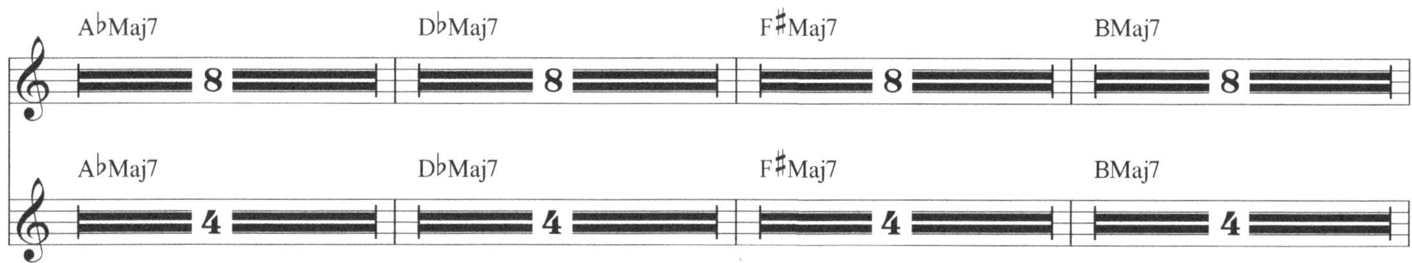

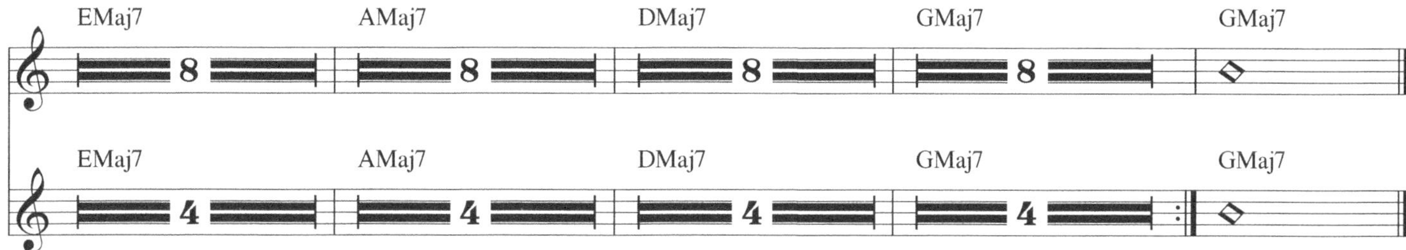

FIG. C.5. Major 7: Eight Bars, Four Bars

Refer to chapter 14 (page 62).

59 – 62

Diminished Major 7

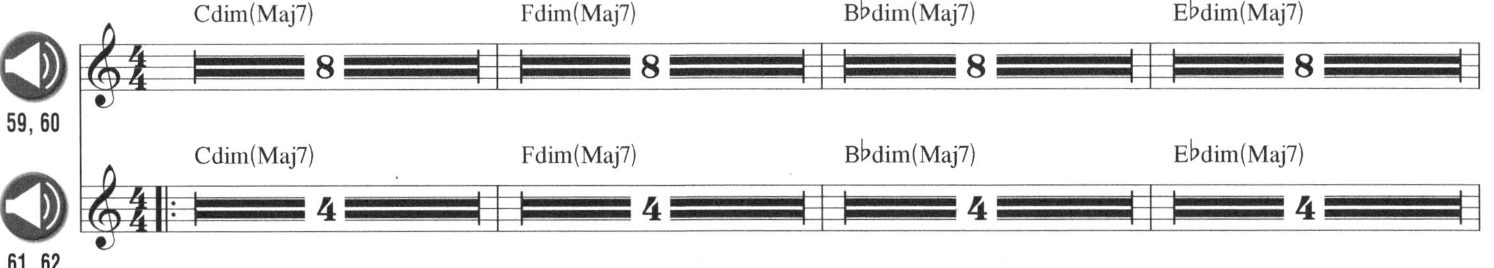

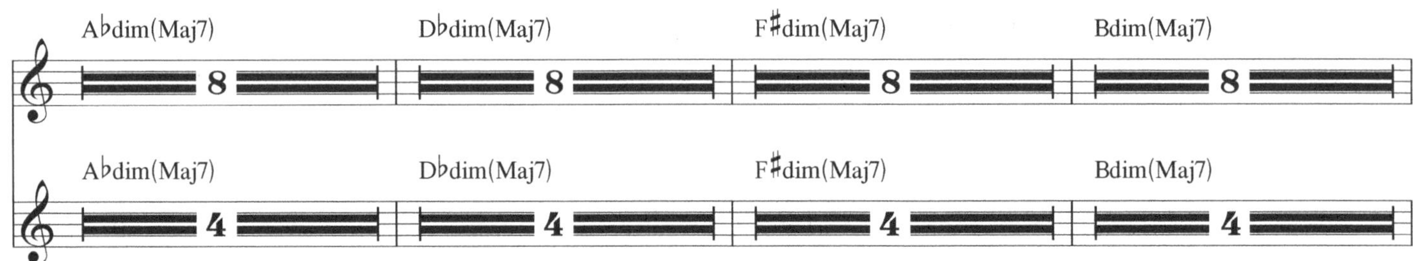

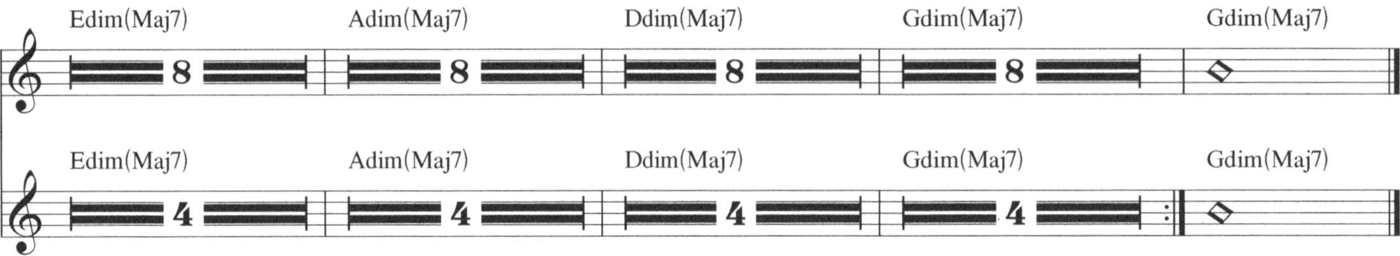

FIG. C.6. Diminished Major 7: Eight Bars, Four Bars

ABOUT THE AUTHOR

Photo by Kelly Davidson

Rick Peckham is an internationally known jazz guitarist and educator. He has presented performances and clinics on six continents and specializes in a unique blend of styles, including jazz, rock, blues, fusion, and country fingerstyle performance.

Currently a full-time professor in Berklee's Guitar Department, Peckham has been a faculty member since 1986. He served as department assistant chair from 1992 to 2013.

Peckham's internationally released album *Left End*, with drummer Jim Black and bassist Tony Scherr, was named one of the best releases of 2005 by *DownBeat* magazine. He organized the college's honorary doctoral tributes to Roy Haynes, Joe Zawinul, Jack DeJohnette, and John Scofield, featuring then-Berklee students Kurt Rosenwinkel, Matthew Garrison, Antonio Hart, Abe Laboriel Jr., Melvin Butler, and Seamus Blake. Berklee students he has coached include Lionel Loueke, Lage Lund, Frank Möbus, Jeff Parker, Matt Stevens, and Nir Felder. In 2018, he served as musical director and producer for *Timeless: A Tribute to John Abercrombie*, that featured Joe Lovano, Joey Baron, Lage Lund, and many Berklee faculty members.

Some of his published works are two twelve-week college courses for Berklee Online: *Berklee Guitar Chords 101* (2007 UCEA award for best online class) and *Berklee Guitar Chords 201*, as well as Berklee Press books *Berklee Jazz Guitar Dictionary* and *Berklee Rock Chord Dictionary*.

For further information regarding upcoming performances and projects, please see **www.rickpeckham.com**.